"In this intensely personal book, Joan Puls shares a part of herself and ultimately helps the reader to do the same...to ask ourselves what compassion is, what it means to pray. In her story we begin to find answers that not only surprise us, but challenge and convince us as well.

"The lives and experiences of real people are presented in a way that allows the reader to see the holiness, the strength, and the conversion within each person. You begin to feel that wholeness and spiritual growth really are possible for anyone with a sincere heart. A double thumbs up to a book that deserves to be read and read again."

The Most Reverend Thomas J. Gumbleton
Auxiliary Bishop of Detroit

"The author urges a compassionate life to heal the wounds in our personal and communal lives."

NC News Service

"Joan Puls recognizes that all of nature is a seamless web, so we can't be casual about evils such as poverty, hunger, and nuclear weapons, no matter what our condition. Yet she doesn't preach or talk down to the reader, so that one has a sense of learning with her about the interconnectedness of things. This is wise counsel, based upon concrete experience, recreated for us in language of simplicity and strength."

Michael True
author of *Justice Seekers, Peacemakers*

Joan Puls identifies displacement, love, community, forgiveness, healing, prayer, and hope as 'outward signs of grace'—sacraments of our time!"

One World

"The wellsprings of the heart are awakened to compassion as one reads this highly autobiographical work. The reader walks with and 'suffers with' the author, as she shares the rich and many experiences of her life and service in the church. Sister Joan has a unique gift of 'telling her story' honestly, humbly, freely."

Agnes Cunningham, S.S.C.M.
Mundelein Seminary

"Taking seven common human experiences, ranging from community to forgiveness, Sr. Joan Puls demonstrates how they provide opportunities to respond in a compassionate way to others."

Catholic New York

A Spirituality of Compassion

JOAN PULS, OSF

TWENTY-THIRD PUBLICATIONS
Mystic, Connecticut

Also by Joan Puls, O.S.F.

Every Bush Is Burning:
A Spirituality for Our Times (1985)

Second printing 1988

Twenty-Third Publications
185 Willow Street
P.O. Box 180
Mystic, CT 06355
(203) 536-2611

ISBN 0-89622-352-3
Library of Congress Catalog Card Number 87-51633

This book is dedicated to all the "links" in the "intersecting circles" in my life, through whom I have learned exchange.

This book is intended for all who are willing to go to the borders and strike the rock, that the waters of life might be released.

CONTENTS

A SPIRITUALITY
OF COMPASSION

INTRODUCTION

I had been on a solitary walk through the Gimel Valley in Switzerland. And I had detoured through the woods to St. Oyen's to enlarge my journey. The road passes a little Reformed church and the words are prominent over the arched doorway. *Je ne mettrai point dehors celui qui me viendra.* (No one who comes to me will I ever reject.) It occurred to me that those words summarize the way it is to be in the life we call Christian, on the journey towards the reign of God. Those few words capture a life given to exchange.

Each of us journeys through the Gimel Valley in search of our souls, on the path of slow and reluctant surrender to God's purposes. Each of us is in exodus, afraid of the commission given us, wandering in our own deserts, arriving at dangerous crossings, tempted by idols. Each of us experiences, at least at critical times, the reassuring sight of cloud and of fire, the faithful presence of God. What is asked of us is that we in turn reject no one. That we go to Pharaoh on behalf of our sisters and brothers. That we trust the power and the presence of God-with-us. That we enter wholeheartedly into a covenant with those who travel with us and become for one another the instruments and signs of God's voice and God's life.

Certain of our encounters and experiences as we travel speak by their very nature of acceptance and exchange. In our prayer, in times of healing and forgiveness, in our encounters in love and in community, in experiences of displacement and of hope, we enter concretely the mystery of God in exchange with us and we in exchange with one another. Our lives and the lives of countless others testify that God is faithful. But it remains our choice to welcome or to reject this faithfulness.

In the Israelites' journey, there was doubt: Is the God we trust in our midst or not? The fibers of their community life were strained by quarreling and recriminations. Why have you led us into this desert? They were exhausted and discouraged, hungry and thirsty. God continued to act through a go-between, Moses, and continued to give signs: the serpent, the parting of the waves, the manna, and water from the rock.

1

When I finished writing *Every Bush Is Burning* on the note of exchange, I knew there was more to be said. "A world of exchange surrounds us. Even though most of the time we fail to perceive it. . . .The secret of spirituality is the uncovering of this life of exchange, this very real and very visible interconnectedness that makes all of creation one. And then finding our own place in the 'flow' of life, entering the mystery and becoming part of the universal 'dance.' Exchange, the dynamic reciprocity that flows between creatures, is the fundamental reality and we all have roles in its patterning and its stream. It is the link between uniqueness and diversity, maximizing both, and setting into motion the plan intended for the world and all that dwells within it."[1] If God is present everywhere, if every bush is burning and our ordinary, daily lives are full of grace, then it is important that we tap our ordinary experiences—strike the rock, so to speak—so that the waters of life might flow.

It will be my endeavor in the pages that follow to explore some of the opportunities you and I have for entering the mystery of exchange and being go-betweens in our personal and communal settings. Displacement, love, community, forgiveness, healing, prayer, and hope are seven outwards signs of inward grace, seven sacraments for our time. In each of them we find ourselves at the borders between separate worlds, faced with the possibility of accepting and exchanging, of striking the rock and unleashing the creative, unifying forces within all of us.

Life is a movement between what is and what is not yet, between slavery and freedom, sin and grace, brokenness and the promise of renewing life. Often it is our wounds that lead us into the deeper places of interchange. We go through our wounds, to the places of purification and repentance, where we are opened to the way of recovery and greater wholeness. We move from the desert of our enclosed egos and self-sufficient existences into the promised land of mutual gifting, where no one need be thirsty. We go to the borders of our lives, not to act as guards, but as go-betweens. We must strike the rock.

ONE

DISPLACEMENT AND DISCIPLESHIP

"Our faith presents us with a fundamental option to choose life or death. I have done all I know how to do over the last four years to bring home to Americans the struggles of Central Americans...I cannot be silent. The legal system does not work for Central Americans, so I cannot ask for anything different. I am prepared to go to prison if that is necessary." [1]

Darlene was in Michigan on retreat when her apartment in Phoenix was searched. A young Salvadoran refugee living with her was apprehended. Darlene had lived and worked in Guatemala with native sisters, creating day-care centers for children in need and ministering pastorally among the poor. A priest they had worked with was killed. The threat of punishment for their work among the poor came too close. Several sisters learned that their names were exposed and their lives in danger. For a time all had to go into exile.

Darlene returned to the United States and quickly became involved with the flow of refugees from Central America. She knew their plight. She had no doubts or misgivings about their motives and their needs. They were fleeing for their lives, for the safety of their families. Darlene's ministry was clear: relo-

3

cating El Salvadorans and Guatemalans in safe places, feeding
and housing them, and attending to their displacement. The refugees in Tucson, Arizona, were not there by choice. They had
left homeland, friends and neighbors unwillingly and under
threat. They had so little means to provide their own reset-
tling. And by U.S. law they were illegal entrants, subject to arrest and deportation. Deportation meant possible, maybe sure,
persecution.

If ever sanctuary was needed, these beleaguered, bewildered and bereaved refugees qualified. Churches in the region
and individuals like Darlene found themselves caught up in a
gospel scene with heavy political overtones. Could it be
against the law to aid and protect helpless people? Do foreign
policies dictate which works of mercy are justified and when?
Could one be judged criminal for guarding the secrets of a family
who had escaped tyranny and sought healing from personal
tragedies? The Sanctuary workers didn't even ask those questions. They responded spontaneously.

In this context of injustice and struggle for human rights, of
persecution and military repression, of exile and forced dependency, of religious conviction and the practice of gospel values,
who defines guilt and criminality? Who judges the motives and
behavior of those escaping torture and those offering sanctuary? Who assesses the priorities of government policy and the
exigencies of human suffering? What judge and what law are to
be the whetstone? By what shifts of fortune and circumstance
do the exiled seek a home in a country where gross numbers of
the population descend from immigrants who also escaped poverty and persecution? And by what shift of fortune do those
who claim the U.S. as their home find themselves exiled within it? It is in the name of freedom that the U.S. enforces its im-
migration laws. Whose freedom?

This is one glimpse of a wound in our world, a wound multiplied and proliferated in other continents and with other nu-
ances. What does it say to us about the times in which we live?
The displaced, the refugees, the homeless, are a universal phenomenon. We watch the scenes being enacted in U.S. courtrooms

and U.S. churches. We watch from afar the starving refugees of the Sudan and Ethiopia. We see the effects of a divided Germany, of the Palestinian situation. We note the continued flow of Arabs and Turks into Europe. Images have developed and multiplied in recent years of refugee camps, resettlement sites, underground transportation systems, migrating tribes, and boat people. The pattern is often the same: people come to a new land seeking a new life. Generations later other people come to those same shores and are rejected, reruns of the human tendency to make claims, then separate and excommunicate. Perhaps the sanctuary movement is one of the most recent "counter" images, a small symbol of reversal and of hope in a world of displaced peoples.

There seems to be a connection between this sign of our time and the Gospel experience of displacement. The very insertion of Jesus into our lives and history was an act of displacement. No clearer description exists than the one in Philippians: "Though he was in the form of God, he did not deem equality with God something to be grasped at. Rather, he emptied himself and took the form of a slave, being born in the likeness of human beings." (2:6-7) Jesus was God-displaced. We call it Incarnation, the Word-made-flesh. John says: "...the world did not know who he was; to his own he came, yet his own did not accept him." (1:10-11)

Jesus' primary mission was to the displaced. In Isaiah's words, applied to himself, he was "sent to bring glad tidings to the poor, to proclaim liberty to captives, recovery of sight to the blind, release to prisoners." (Luke 4:18) They are still with us: the poor, captives, the blind, prisoners. Jesus came to give his life as ransom. Jesus' displacement became a point of ridicule as he approached that ultimate moment of ransom. All hail, king of the Jews, chanted the soldiers. You are a king of sorts and so we clothe you in a purple cloak and a crown of thorns. We bow before you mockingly. Your kingship is not authentic; you are a displaced king.

Jesus explicitly invited all of us to live the way of displacement. It is the displaced whom he names "blessed" in that famous sermon. It is they who are eligible for God's realm, indeed, who are experiencing that realm-in-its-coming: the poor in spirit, the sorrowing, the meek, the persecuted, the peacemakers. That sermon is a textbook for those who would see into and through this sign of our times, finding direction and instruction for their response. The homeless of our world and the upheavals we witness in creation are signs of broken covenants, signs of our failure to recognize one another as members of our human family and our role as stewards and caretakers of the earth's resources.

How do we turn failure into a new covenant? How do we renew a sense of solidarity and relatedness between ourselves and the displaced of our world? Re-open the path of exchange between exploiter and exploited, victim and oppressor? Reestablish a harmony between creation and those who abuse it? As we look at contemporary situations of upheaval and uprootedness and examine their effects on our own lives, we are led to ask: What response is required of Christians and disciples? What do we learn from the many-faceted experiences of displacement about new patterns of solidarity and exchange?

These are the responses I propose in this chapter: 1) the beatitudes suggest a process of inner displacement; 2) desert experiences scour our souls and strip us of false identities; 3) identification with those who are poor schools us in solidarity and enables us to cross to the borders; 4) becoming missionaries in our contemporary world means removing our blinders and opening ourselves to others' gifts; 5) each moment of letting go, exch experience of dying, advances our gradual displacement and adapts us to life at the crossroads. Discipleship guarantees displacement, and displacement will re-model and renew our spirituality.

DISPLACEMENT: A SIGN OF OUR TIMES

My country's history is the tale of immigrants and of pioneers, voluntary in most instances, and representing a quest for freedom and new horizons. Many of our ancestors rejoiced in their good fortune to board a ship and sail to havens of tolerance and new opportunities. But we North Americans can never evade the haunting truth of the Native Americans' displacement.

The history of their oppression, neglect, and destruction as a people reads as a detailed list of sins and broken commitments and ends as a burden of guilt which we don't even dare address. They are homeless, having lost their culture, their land, their pride, their hope, because we have displaced them, blatantly and smugly. That wound on our soil and our national conscience refuses to go away. We are a vivid example of the displaced displacing another people.[2]

Such clouds have hung heavy over the centuries in various parts of the world, and the sea of suffering humanity has swelled. Civil wars and wars between nations, injustice and repression, hunger and hostility, have driven Afghanistans, Polish and German Jews, Indians and Pakistanis, Haitians and Cubans, Latin Americans and South Pacific Islanders into the oceans and onto the barbed wire encampments of our day, forced them to risk everything crossing desert and guarded boundaries, and deposited them in slums and barrios unfit for human dwelling.

Our awareness of these moving masses has been heightened by the ways they touch each of us in our own setting. We in the U.S. recently celebrated the 200th anniversary of our Statue of Liberty. Despite the million-dollar repairs and the expensive galas associated with its "restoration," "celebration" was an ironical misnomer for many. There is no liberty for those "huddled masses" who come from the "wrong" part of the world. Recent and personal experiences of unemployment and economic insecurity prevent many in the U.S. from opening their arms in welcome to southern neighbors. They regard them solely as competitors for scarce jobs, and as liabilities for the welfare and social service systems. Needy refugees become threats to those recently established and still struggling upward. Hatred and disregard for life in one country yield to persecution and suspicion in the new country. Is it any wonder that the displaced see no way sometimes but to become preyers themselves? I have long been aware of the homeless poor in Milwaukee. St. Ben's Loaves and Fishes Program has brought bag ladies, down-and-out alcoholics, and the mentally disturbed into clear focus for me in a way that regularly disturbs my complacency and niggles at my conscience. How did they get there? I often ask. The twin sisters, one of whom is blind. John, the gigantic Indian, respected by his street companions in spite of his habit of drunkenness. Bill, the gentle, shy, smiling man with a beard, who could certainly qualify as a Santa Claus. Their dignity shines through their layers of cast-off clothing and hesitant eyes. How did they get there? This is the affluent west. This is a provident community in a stable country in peacetime. One begins to realize the relative meaning of provident and stable and peacetime.

What is the story of their displacement? What factors caused their uprooting and exile, and reduced them to the dependency of street beggars and addicts? Do they willingly walk the way to State Street and free handouts, emergency shelters and jail cells? I doubt it.

If we dare, we can come even closer, into our own community and family circles, and recognize displacement on the faces of those around us. The men who share the pews with us who once stood at our altars and in our pulpits. We call them resigned priests. Would it not be more correct to call them displaced? And the elderly who shrivel away in tiny rooms in our low-cost housing projects and nursing homes. Displaced by infirmity, by lack of means and failing energies, destined to stare out windows at the life they left behind, or to live behind bolted doors in fear and loneliness. The victims of AIDS. A new law in the U.S. would allow employers to dismiss those who have AIDS under certain conditions. AIDS victims are ostracized and displaced, along with all society's undesirables and unwanteds. The levels of homelessness and displacement are multiple and each of us knows, in our flesh or in our social sensitivity, the sting and the stigma.

Displaced persons are perhaps the most glaring statistic of our times. The categories of the marginal grow, internationally, nationally, even denominationally. What about the displaced homosexuals, displaced women who seek a place of dignity and responsibility in the church, the divorced, those excommunicated for sundry reasons and according to frail human judgments?

In our times creation itself is subject to violent displacement. Two examples suffice. In many places the very existence of the land is being threatened. Small farmers are forced to yield their dreams and lifelong investments to the encroaching expansion of agribusiness. Not only are thousands of family farmers in the U.S. today in the process of being uprooted, the land itself is being converted into technological and economical entities bent on profit, and not necessarily on the best use of the resource, earth. Strip-mining has carelessly usurped precious land, robbing it and its caretakers. Development, that abstract but all-consuming giant, has claimed meadow and marsh for its own purposes: cement parks, high-rise dwellings and barren blocks of look-alike buildings. I bemoan the dearth of wild flowers in my native U.S. when I see the plenitude of variety and color in Europe. At the same time I meet in England the same warning signs that confront U.S. citizens: "Nuclear dump sites" and "Leukemia is claiming our children."

The consequences of the displacement of nature, the thwarting of creation, are rootlessness and alienation for present and future generations. "It is difficult to undo our own damage, and to recall to our presence that which we have asked to leave. It is hard to desecrate a grove and change your mind. . . .We doused the burning bush and cannot rekindle it. . . .Now speech has perished from among the lifeless things of earth, and living things say very little to very few."[3]

Before we have finished with exhausting and contaminating the earth's resources, prompting multiple displacements, we have begun our attack on space. We have "progressed" from exploration and scientific discovery to the misuse and calculated exploitation of space. From being a symbol of the spirit and its dreams and vast expanses, space is currently being co-opted as the symbol of the most far-reaching and irresponsible war yet designed. We will not be content until we have endangered the entire planet earth from a perverse system set somewhere among the stars. One has the sense of a demonic race to "displace" anything in creation that is innocent and vulnerable (perhaps even God), usually under tall names like defense, progress, technological breakthrough, the protection of national interests, etc. There are even attempts to displace in the name of peace.

Simpler minds perhaps, those given to the search for God's purposes in our world and for a more comprehensively harmonious view of reality, would use other terms. Evil is the failure of beings to function according to their nature. Sin is the misuse of creation and of human energies. Violence occurs when respect and reverence for life and created things are replaced by neglect, misuse, or attack. As human beings we have failed to understand and obey the laws of God, of human community, of nature itself. Displacement is one of the results of that failure.

As I contemplate this world-reality, the wounds of displacement, the dead-end patterns of oppressed and oppressor, I sit in a three hundred-year-old converted stable in Norfolk, England. The cottage attached is surrounded by garden and field, a harmonious environment speaking of security and continuity. From our personal experiences we resonate easily and deeply with the word "home." Perhaps not the same images as our grandparents, but family celebrations, nostalgic reunions, handed-down furniture, inherited land, heirlooms and treasures. "Our town" is no less real than it was for Thornton Wilder. We have our familiar streets and stores and our special memories. No matter how critical we become of our country's policies and its leaders, we ache for news from home when we are abroad, and we feel the tinge of pride when other nations applaud or ally with us. We want to be proud of the place that gave us birth, nurtured us, and sent us forth. That "we" is universal and human. Part of our identity is contained in the people and places that constitute our particular world.

Some years ago Alvin Toffler's *Future Shock* reminded us that our world was changing, rapidly and radically. Society is mobile to the extreme, with subsequent effects on relationships and attitudes. Interest grew in tracing one's roots and establishing one's ethnicity. For more and more of us there was no one place in our lives. We moved necessarily if not comfortably among many places. We surrendered some of our more traditional notions of belonging and rootedness. But the movement into double careers and condominiums and less permanent relationships did not mean displacement. Most of us held firm to those center poles that determine for us the heart and bedrock of our acceptance and our happiness. Family perhaps, or career, church affiliation, or a sense of our own search and fulfillment. We believe we are franchised, that we belong, and have open opportunity and some degree of security. Home is something we are still assured of. Most of us do not experience the ruthless uprooting, the total loss of security, the dangerous flight into the unknown. Some of us glimpse the upheavals associated with displacement when we mourn a loved one, undergo bankruptcy, work through a divorce or broken relationship, or adapt to the gradual loss of our physical mobility. We are often guilty of a cruel innocence, as we read about mass movements in Africa, or watch scenes of camp squalor in Honduras. We rest in a false security, in the knowledge that we have built barns for the future. We cannot imagine, and shirk from facing, the possibility of our earth-home being destroyed by nuclear warfare.

We don't deny that this worldwide, all-embracing phenomenon of displacement and uprooting is one of the signs of our times. If we are serious Christians, we reject the double-talk and glossing over of our ministers of defense, our development planners, our amoral and agnostic technicians and technocrats. We reject the excessive nationalism of our foreign policy and the aggressive hostilities generated between political entities. We reaffirm our belief in the possibility of a covenant between human beings and nature, between persons of different races and political and religious outlooks. We admit our complicity with the systems of greed and ambition. We believe, however weakly and ineffectively, in exchange in the very realms where we see the violation of creation and the displacement of people. We try to imagine alternatives to the patterns that seem to surround and perpetuate these tragedies. We approach the question of discipleship and the displacement that it implies.

BEATITUDES AND INNER DISPLACEMENT

"Blessed are the lowly; they shall inherit the land. Blessed are the sorrowing; they shall be consoled." (Matthew 5:4-5) To take the beatitudes as our guide is to allow a revolution in our consciousness whereby we move closer to the pain and plight of those who have been left out of life and its decisions and benefits. We come to some identity with them through taking on some of the experiences from which they cannot escape. We do it from the inside so that our external life can gradually approximate a likeness to theirs. We enter their burdens and discover a unity with them, not only for the sake of solidarity in suffering, but as a foundation for exchange, a shifting of the weight of oppression, a sign of our willingness to embody the values which our world has rejected. We endeavor to enable those values to speak again to those who will listen, and to point the way toward new relationships in society.

It will be a revolution, costly, disruptive, risky. We will have to do it unilaterally, not depending on "the other side" to meet us halfway or to applaud our goodwill gestures. If we are to be merciful, we can't be selective. If we want to be peacemakers, it is a full-time commitment. If we accept persecution, we can't do our own prosecuting. Jesus' taking flesh was a unilateral movement. It was a choice for vulnerability. Jesus didn't try on his human condition or rehearse the path of his crucifixion, with the option of changing his mind. Discipleship guarantees displacement.

We will have to begin a divestment process. Each of us knows what are the created things and the objects of our possessiveness that block and blind us. Each of us knows the recognition we need, the positions of distinction we can't yet surrender, the security which we resist yielding. We know our phobia for failure and our reluctance to admit doubt and weakness. Each of us shrinks from the vulnerability of pain and powerlessness. We are uncomfortable in the presence of another's naked grief and we lack courage to reveal our own. We prefer to mourn in private or to repress the awful pangs of mourning and loss that rack our inner beings.

Each of us wants instinctively to be in control. To be self-sufficient, to determine our lives, even its details. To be in command of present operations and future plans. We fight back unprompted when challenged and feel resentment at the slightest offense. We will have to lay down our arms and surrender our defenses. Let go of territory around or within us that we have conquered or won. It will be "against the grain," and against long-cultivated habits, to embrace the way of the beatitudes. T.S. Eliot said it starkly: "In order to arrive at what you do not know, you must go by a way which is the way of ignorance. In order to possess what you do not possess, you must go by the way of dispossession. In order to arrive at what you are not, you must go through the way in which you are not."[4] To arrive at displacement we must go the way of displacement. Yet we do this in response to a call and as integral to our discipleship, so that, in Nouwen's words, actual displacements become the places where we hear God's message and discover God's purposes and patterns for human community.[5]

THE DESERT AND ITS STRIPPING

"Jesus was led into the desert by the Spirit." (Matthew 4:1) The way of solitude, fasting and discipline, replacing noise, creature comforts and carnal pleasure. The call to withdraw and to be tested. The call to conversion and inner transformation. Only when our immediate life-supports collapse do we know with some degree of certainty on what our stability ultimately rests.

The poustinia movement is designed to strip the retreatant of the usual props and comforts and allow him or her to come to terms with emptiness and a certain displacement. But often we don't have to go into a preplanned desert. Life offers its own desert experiences.

For me there were three years of fatigue and emotional numbness leading into depression, prompting a deep inner dismantling and a slow and agonizing renovating. It was the last way I would have chosen. I had just completed my doctorate and stood at the entrance of a long-awaited career as a philosophy professor. I had survived Hegelian abstractions, the tedium of research and degree requirements, and the crisis of dissertation orals. The classroom was now my "kingdom," open minds my acreage, and a Ph.D. my insignia. But I found myself on a spiral which stripped me naked, forced me into a crouch, and sucked me into a narrow tunnel of emotional paralysis and black depression. There, in that place, in my displacement, I sat and waited and worried. "What you do not know is the only thing you know."[6] I did not know if I had a future; the past had been snatched away. I was on the fringes of any human community I had ever known, a subject of discussion and analysis, an object of pity and compassion. Few dared to enter my tunnel and share my doubts and despair. The desert closed around me and stretched out to the farthest reaches of my existence, dry and barren and defeating.

Today I claim that period of my life as sacred. As time for the old to die and the new to be born, the mighty to be fallen and the lowly to be lifted up, the way opened for an understanding and a sensitivity and a hope that can include the most forlorn and the most broken of human beings. "To arrive where you are, you must go by a way wherein there is no ecstasy."[7] Having been displaced, from my personal and professional roots, and finding myself in a mental ward, on the roster of the useless, there are many things I can never again take for granted, and many things I no longer value in the same way. I was reduced to the lowest level of human existence. There I took possession of my humanity and a common humanity in a way I can never regret. The question remains, twenty years later: How do I walk from this desert into others' deserts and point the way toward new shoots of life? How can my experience be gift, not only for me, but for those in tunnels of their own and others' choosing? How can my "exodus" benefit others?

Thomas Merton describes the monk as "a marginal person who withdraws deliberately...with a view to deepening fundamental human experience."[8] How do modern monks, modern Christians, achieve this withdrawal and gain this perspective on their complex and involved lives, so that they can interpret the messages and enticements of an idolatrous world and know to whom they wish to give their allegiance; so that others can share the fruit of the inner freedom they have gained?

FINDING OUR WAY TO THE BORDERS

"The foxes have lairs, the birds in the sky have nests, but the Human One has nowhere to lay his head." (Matthew 8:20) The way of divestment, insecurity, downward mobility, replacing property, status, and possessions. The call to risk, to move closer to the periphery of society. We either make clear and concrete our solidarity with those at the margin or we live in the mists between the gospel and our need for human respect.

We have signposts for this way. In the footsteps of Dorothy Day long streams of Catholic workers have crossed to the borders, in cities all across the United States. Dorothy Day refused to separate Jesus from his homelessness, his poverty, his cross. "To help the organizers, to give what you have for relief, to pledge yourself to voluntary poverty for life so that you can share with your brothers (and sisters) is not enough. One must live with them, share with them their sufferings too. Give up one's privacy, and mental and spiritual comforts as well as physical."[9]

Jean Vanier and his followers in the L'Arche movement cross family and social lines to associate with some of the neediest members of society, the mentally handicapped. Under the inspiration of Charles de Foucauld, the Brothers and Sisters of Jesus have chosen displacement, living in small groups in the poorest and most deprived neighborhoods, enduring the same insecurity and gruelling labor as the people whose lives they share. Insertion into the wounds and way of life of the marginalized. Utter involvement in the human condition. Links, by words and example, to others who might be open to their own divestment and to new modes of sharing.

Certainly Dorothy Day has pricked the conscience of many, including those in high ecclesiastical places. She could become, if those ardent about the cause of her sainthood persevere, the newest patron of the displaced and the marginal. Jean Vanier's words have punctured many armors of middle class and insulated Christians. And the witness of groups like Foucauld's followers offer a challenge to all who would test the waters of an option for the poor. But they arrived there by the way of displacement, actual physical involvement and voluntary uprooting from their own potentially secure lives and careers.

For many of us it is a test even to be identified with the

downcast and the weak of our world. We lack the courage to approach the lepers on our streets and offer even minor assistance. We lack the courage to step out into the unknown, giving up a respectable job, a good salary, title, and assured recognition. In even small ways, and when risks are minimal, we tend to choose our companions by their respectability, our routes by their protection from unpleasant sights and sounds, and our churches by their relative freedom from a serious gospel thrust.

I remember, with wry amusement now, the day I sat in an alcove of the mental hospital, with a book open on my lap. A visitor joined me and we were having a semi-awkward conversation about hospital events and "outside" activities. Then a group of student nurses came onto the floor, guided by a supervisor elaborating on the programs and therapies of the "inmates." My visitor was visibly uncomfortable. I understood why when I realized she might be mistaken as the patient. She in no way wanted to be me.

We in no way want to be those who are unacceptable. No wonder society's unacceptables remain so far at the fringes! Who will be the interpreters, the bridge between them? Who will verify the humanity and the interdependence of us all? Who will help to balance the scales of compassion and of justice?

MISSIONARY FORMATION

"Who is my mother? Who are my brothers?" The way of openness and inclusivity, replacing stereotypes and insularity, with their rigid boundaries. The call to cross over, to expand and integrate, to break through categories and to disturb clubhouse mentalities. Who is my mother, who are my brothers? Questions to be asked by Christians in South Africa, in racially troubled areas in the U.S., among the static hostilities in Ireland, by Baptists and Roman Catholics in ecumenically-barren areas of any country.

Simone Weil was Jewish and French. She was of frail health, intelligent, from a well-to-do family. Though a teacher, she had a strong sense of solidarity with factory workers. She loved St. Francis and Gregorian chant. Without leaving her involvements in the secular political world, she sought guidance for her new-found faith. She remained forever on the threshold, never baptized, never formally a Christian. Eventually she took on the life of a peasant, working in the vineyards, and sending donations to political prisoners. It was said of her that she believed we should love people in the same way that the sun loves us, gratuitously and universally.[10] She was someone at home at the borders. She was a point of contact between mathematics and Marxism, Judaism and Christianity, ancient philosophy and mysticism, the upper class and the worker.

Perhaps she is a model for all would-be missionaries. We understand better now, after much revising of our missiologies, the meaning of mutuality. We are less keen on bringing God into new places, or taking God captive in our cultural images, and more aware of the work of the Spirit underway in all places and through all peoples. Only an appreciation for the gifts of others entitles missionaries an entrance into the private lives and personal beliefs of others. Each of us goes into new areas with empty hands and open hearts or we pose an obstacle to the Spirit's own exchange, to our mutual discovery and growth. Until we lose our rigid codes of belonging and our exclusive criteria for membership, we multiply boundaries rather than create potential bonds.

What is it that most accurately describes the missionary in our times? Not physical hardships, nor the likelihood of martyrdom, though they are not necessarily excluded. Vincent Donovan, a missionary to the Masai in Tanzania for seventeen years, says: "A missionary is essentially a social martyr, cut off from his roots, his stock, his blood, his land, his background, his culture. He is destined to walk forever a stranger in a strange land. He must be stripped as naked as a human being can be, down to the very texture of his (or her) being."[11] A transcultural vision that removes our blindnesses and our blocks. A humbler view of the riches of our own heritage (whether that be nationality, denomination, religious spirit), recognizing the richness of the human race in all its diversity. We must decrease, so that the gifts and contributions of others can increase.

Sister Darlene said in her court testimony prior to her sentencing for her role in Sanctuary: "I do not know what else to do to make concrete my solidarity and oneness with my suffering brothers and sisters of Central America. . . .We have not done anything to warrant a sentence, but neither have the Central Americans who remain detained in camps here in the U.S. I do not want any special treatment."

I repeated that phrase in essence many times as I prepared for my second extended journey to India. And I voiced it often to the sisters with whom I lived in central and south India. I do not want any special treatment. Your ways are to be mine while I am here. I want to share your hardships and discomforts. During those three months in 1986 I experienced the weight of those words. And was forced to admit my inability to be so thoroughly displaced. What I wanted and what I could endure were two different things. I understood better the glib words of the disciples: we will not leave you.

When I landed in Coimbatore, weary and sick, I secretly hoped that a car would be there to take me the last sixty minutes of the journey. I didn't want the privilege of riding in an insufferably hot, over-crowded bus. When prayer began each morning in the tiny chapel and temperatures were already in the nineties, I wanted the special treatment of an overhead fan, with my stool placed directly beneath it. When rice and curry and vegetables were served, monotonously and in forms completely foreign to my taste buds, I looked hungrily for the special side-dishes of fried potatoes and boiled bananas. Even for three months I was not up to the rigors of displacement. I felt it most keenly when I became ill, with dysentery and dehydration. I accepted without question whatever special treatment was available, even the luxury of a room that caused the displacement of four young sisters. Very quickly in India I learned how difficult it was, in spite of my motivation and intent, to overcome fifty years of comfortable living, constant choice, and familiar conveniences. We learn slowly the meaning of inclusivity and transcultural openness.

LEARNING TO DIE

"Unless the grain of wheat falls to the earth and dies, it remains just a grain of wheat. But if it dies, it produces much fruit." (John 12:24) The way of surrender and letting go, of abandonment to the purpose and rhythms of life. The call to turn diminishment and suffering into fruitfulness and compassion.

As I write these pages, my sister-in-law is dying of cancer. Five years ago she was confronted with breast cancer, a mastectomy, and chemotherapy treatments. She weathered those and attempted to return to normal life, her part-time job, and her grandchildren. Then another dark reality, bone and lung cancer, inoperable and unresponsive to various and continued treatments. I visited her before I went to India and she spoke of her losing battle and approaching death. A homebody herself, she entered wholeheartedly into my forthcoming adventures. Before I left, she proposed an exchange. Write to me when you can, she said, and I'll offer some of my suffering for your mission. It was a deepening of the bond we had had previously. Whenever we enter with another that mystery of exchange and substitution, mutual sharing of burdens, we find ourselves in a new relationship. Now seven months later, she is still en route to that final displacement. And her physical diminishment, with its concomitant pain, is still bearing fruit.

This spring a forty-one-year-old friend of mine died suddenly in a freak car accident. She was on her way to a prayer service following the U.S. bombings of Tripoli in Libya. She was also at the time on a visit of support to those convicted of Sanctuary "crimes." And she was returning from a parish in New Mexico where she was searching out a possible ministry. Pat's entire life was a commitment to the poor and to peace. She lived and worked in a hospitality house in Milwaukee's inner city. She spent whatever time she could at peace demonstrations and vigils, praying and fasting, denouncing policies of war and greed and violence. Twice she had been jailed for acting on her beliefs. She had the freedom of a true disciple, and the simplicity of an authentic Franciscan. She died as such, another step in her course of voluntary displacement. And each of us who knew her, and were bruised and caressed by her ardent spirit, experienced the fruit of her life. My own present journey into the mysteries of nonviolence, and its far-flung implications, has been quickened and heightened by Pat's abiding spirit.

It is not only through the loss of life that the miracle of new life happens. Each scenario of letting go and being displaced is the site of a new harvest and of new hope. A friend of mine has given up an honored position, the acclaim of a wide segment of church leaders, and the security attached, to enter a period of search about her own future. A parish priest has resigned from his ministry in a developing parish to make way for new leadership and to bring his accumulated experience to a new ministry in hospice work.

We see as well the sad results of "hanging on," of refusing to step aside and to surrender to the tides of time. Persons who no longer have the imagination and energy for the position they hold. Persons who offer their successors only negative criticism. Those who become turned in and bitter because they cannot bear the loss of prestige and influence.

Each of us knows something of the dying demanded in our close personal relationships. The more intense our commitments and the greater the investments we have made, the more costly the personal sacrifices. The more cherished and honored the loved one, the more disappointing and shattering the inevitable betrayals and infidelities. A lasting and deep relationship calls for diverse displacements. Either they bear fruit in a common mission and a deeper trust, or they turn inward, poisoning the very life they are part of. When we love another, we give that person a power he or she would not otherwise have. Vanstone says: "The power over itself which love gives to its object may be described in various ways. It is power to make angry or to make glad...to frustrate or to fulfill, to determine tragedy or triumph...he [or she] who loves surrenders into other hands the issue and outcome of his own aspiration—its denouement as triumph or tragedy."[12] That vulnerability and risk represent a dying. Without it, the joy and fulfillment and fruit of love cannot emerge. With it appears also the pain of suspense and the possibility of displacement.

These places of dying and letting go, provided by our choices to love and to risk, and by the natural processes of sickness, aging and death, are training arenas for discipleship. We yearn to pray as did Chardin: "Grant that I may recognize you under the species of each alien or hostile force that seems bent upon destroying or uprooting me...grant that I may understand that it is you who are painfully parting the fibers of my being in order to penetrate to the very marrow of my substance and bear me away within yourself."[13] We yearn to be readied for the complete displacement of ourselves, our sin, our ego, our stubborn refusal to be created anew, so that we may be made fruitful for the purposes of life itself.

Those who believe in a process of displacement, after the manner of the gospel and in harmony with the mystery of death and life, will wrestle with God repeatedly, as did Jacob. And most of us will find ourselves limping. The sufficiency of grace, and the inability of displacement to separate us from the source and grounding of our life, are experiences we recognize only after the fact. "In order to get from where you are now, you must go by a way wherein there is no ecstasy."[14] In the end, we only know whether we can drink the common cup of suffering after we have willingly lifted it to our lips.

THERE IS NO ONE BUT US

The wounds of displacement cause pain in our social body and in our human spirits. They can lead us to hear the gospel's call to diminishment and to solidarity. We can become signs of healing and places of reunion for the dislocated people of our world.

Today's disciples are called to live more consciously within the paradoxes of the Christian life. To live detached lives in the midst of all our attachments. To remain intimately connected to country, to church, to one's own local community, while distancing oneself enough to critique the same. To renounce certain goods and advantages for the sake of a more total possession of oneself and of creation. "To live simply so that others may simply live" and to surrender excessive ambition and society's standards of success in order to share the life and values of those who must struggle and resist. To immerse oneself in the human condition, its pains and potential, in order to emerge more cognizant of its needs. To allow our personal displacements to open our eyes to the brokenness of us all, to the need for healing and for community. To redefine what is permanent and secure in our lives so that we can pilgrim with others, finding our strength and our insurance in their company. To go freely to the byways and crossroads where we are more likely to meet the sons and daughters of a displaced God.

We don't want to minimize the plight of the homeless. We don't want to glorify the pilgrim life. We want to acknowledge that all of us, falsely secure, insisting on control, climbing our own ladders and pushing others aside in the process, are also victims of displacement. And that we who profess our Christian beliefs are professing our willingness to live among the dispersed as one of them. "Christians," says the second-century epistle to Diognetus, "are not distinguished from the rest of humankind either in locality or in speech or in customs...they dwell in their own countries but only as sojourners...and they endure all hardships as strangers."[15] Can we find our center of gravity no matter where we happen to be, at home or abroad, among friends or strangers, in hard times and in times of abundance?

We look around for those whose lives transcend the petty divisions and boundaries of nationhood, sect, and social class. People who recognize the false faces, and speak the true names, of selfishness and sin. People who sift through the debris to find the hidden shoots of hope and heroism. We need the Desmond Tutus who belong to all of South Africa, the Sanctuary workers who expect to share the lot of the refugees, the truly ecumenical who view the whole inhabited world as their mission and their home. We need the contemplatives in the world, people who dare to live on the margins of society, who are not dependent on social acceptance, and who prefer a kind of free-floating existence under a state of risk. We need the ordinary Christians who resist the tendency to settle into a false comfort and a false security. We need those who believe in community,

communities that cross all possible lines, authentic communities
that are the church of our day, and who accept displacement as
a necessary step to our unity. If we believe the gospel, we affirm
the truth that we are one and the illusion that we are not. We
need presidents and pastors and professionals and pioneers who
believe together in the new earth where "they shall live in
the houses they build and eat the fruit of the vineyards they
plant...where they shall not toil in vain, nor beget children for
sudden destruction." (Isaiah 65:21, 23, 25) We need them all.
But there is only us. "There is no one to send...but only us, a gen-
eration comforting ourselves with the notion that we have come
to an awkward time...we ourselves unfit, not yet ready. . . .But
there is no one but us. There never has been."[16]

We are to become, personally and incarnationally, the
place where displacement is reversed. In our private lives and
in the circles we inhabit. In our life of prayer and in all our ministry, we are to be "centers of replacement." Open to the cries
and curses of the uprooted and the plunderers. Aware of the ag-
onies of both victims and those who sentence them. Seeking in
our own hearts the compassion that God extends unqualifiedly
to all in the human family. We can become sacred ground
whereon those of opposite character may meet and not be oblit-
erated. Sanctuaries for those needing refuge or respite or renewal. All that is possible for a community at prayer. I have felt
that atmosphere being breathed at certain moments, in ecumenical circles especially. Prayer experiences where no one is excommunicated. Because all are aware that we share a
fundamental condition of weakness and incompleteness. That
we are all interconnected in our responsibility for the pain that
consumes us.

We are to be missionaries at home and away from home. Interpreters and translators, go-betweens for those who do not
speak each other's languages nor yet know the value of each other's gifts. A living link between the "haves" and "have-nots,"
however real or imaginary those riches and however misjudged
the poverty. Between the bishop who is displaced from ordinary
earthly affairs and the people who are displaced from their

rightful place in the church. Between the people who search life's meaning from the fullness of their experience and the vicars who are empty of self-knowledge and humility.

We must find our way to the margins of society. Making ourselves more useless in order to restore balance to current standards of usefulness. Making ourselves outsiders to appreciate the needs of those who are elitist. Associating with undesirables to understand their long dehumanizing journey and its resultant despair. Taking sides with the exiled and the aliens to relativize human laws and judgments. Eating with publicans and sinners to discover the substance of Jesus' own preferential option for the poor.

We must offer ourselves as places of hospitality and exchange. Letting go of personal wounds to welcome the one who symbolizes our displacement. Turning our physical pain into opportunities for our own and other's growth. Converting brokenness into forgiveness and healing, and failures into expanded sight and sensitivity. Losing some of our prejudices and opening ourselves to new truths. Replacing our need for recognition and honor with anonymous and uncelebrated solidarity.

Just as the journey away from unity and human community goes by way of forced displacement, so does the journey back to solidarity and unity go by way of voluntary displacement. Is it possible that only the combined voluntary displacements (in their multiple forms) of sincere Christians and seekers can heal this wound of our society? Is it at least true that the gospel calls you and me to accept displacement and to choose it in order to reestablish the true meaning of security and of belonging? It will take intense effort and imagination and will to solve these deeply-rooted social problems. But we need signs to help point the way.

TWO

LOVE AND RISK

*"This comes with great love, and sorrow for all the pain
I've caused. . . .I am conscious of much terrain traversed
and of being wiser in our loving, of a deeper acceptance of
each other's limitations, and an honoring of each other
in our uniqueness and our desire to be faithful."*

In his living and dying, Jesus absorbed all that was human.
He exposed himself to poverty, to the vacillations of human
companionship, to the torture of self-doubt, and to the risk of
rejection. J.V. Taylor says: "What we learn about God in Jesus
Christ must include both the inexhaustible activity of Galilee,
redemptive and life-giving, and the silent passivity of the
passion, hands tied and at the disposal of others."[1] Are there
more powerfully poignant words in the gospels than John's "to
his own he came, yet his own did not accept him"? The ultimate failure in human interaction is rejection.

An infant child, unable to reason and interpret, is perma-
nently scarred by parental neglect. The physically handicapped hear the echoes of insensitive remarks for long years.
Human failures in marriage, in partnerships, in family circles,
entail a double loss: self-esteem and the security of those settings. Discarded lovers, husbands whose alcoholism made them

intolerable, women whose glamor and attractiveness faded, the mentally ill who cause embarrassment and hardship, all become castoffs, no longer qualifying, no longer wanted. Displacement, by those who were home and family and friend, dehumanizes the has-been and leaves him or her without a ground or a sense of direction. He or she falls out of the structures and supports that made life manageable and meaningful, and slips or plunges into a kind of nothingness, into non-being.

"He came to his own and his own did not accept him." Worse even, he gave his life on their behalf, and they were not even remorseful. As long as we have time, to resolve a relationship, to put right our brokenness and alienation, there is hope. Even over great distances of time and space we have a chance to be reunited and that chance sustains and enlivens us. As long as neither the possibility of contact nor the wound of distorted love has totally closed, all is not lost. But you and I have heard, if not experienced, the finality in those words: She died and I did not have time to tell her I loved her. Or, he left and we never gathered up our unresolved lives. Or, if I had cared, she might still be alive today. Endless self-questioning, eternal regrets.

It is presumptuous of me to write about love. And yet it is necessary and right for me to do so. If life is whole, and nothing is alien to our spiritual journey, then love, with all its human expressions, is a subject for reflection. Human life is lived in relationship, and love is the essential experience of exchange. 1) It places us in the rhythm of the cosmos, locates us in the stream of human exchange. 2) It makes us vulnerable and prompts us to lives of "substitution." 3) It matures us, stretching us beyond our selfish inclinations and limits. 4) It illuminates the multi-dimensionality of life. 5) It reveals and unleashes hidden powers. 6) It evades us and lures us into dangerous freedoms. Those are the facets of love to be explored in this chapter.

LIFE IS EXCHANGE

For those who believe, exchange is the secret of the universe. Not only humans, but all reality exists in relationship. Chardin pioneered new understanding of this truth. Today's physicists are revealing far-flung facets of this vast, intricate world of mutual interaction and connectedness. History itself is a web of relationships. No age can be separated from another. The past and the present and the future are interwoven, by individual and communal deeds and destinies. Time itself contains a dimension of eternity. World events jolt us into the recognition that we are but one people on one planet, acting out our lives with mutual consequences. The stage on which we perform is limited and what happens in one corner of the world resounds in our own. From the most artificial form of exchange—currency— to the multiple media for communication, we submit to the truth of our interrelatedness. Occasionally we get illuminated flashes of this hidden reality. For Christians the Eucharist supremely opens up the mystery of life exchanged.

Behind the facades of our distinct existences and our separated realms of self and nation, we tiny human specimens are participants in a dance. With the cosmic dance as our supporting background, the music of the universe plays. The dance is compelling. We lead and we follow, in a polyphony of movements and rhythms. Life, when it is vital and creative, is reaching out and receiving, matching strides, over against, an endless series of meetings and goings forth, of finding and letting go, each one free, each one part of the pattern. We may barely touch as we move through life's spaces, but we are all partners in this dance. Our connectedness is the source of our growth and our greatness. We are defined by the life we exchange, one with another, from the first moments of tentative, embryonic existence, to the final slipping away of our breath and being. "We are put on earth a little space, that we may learn to bear the beams of love."[2]

As plants innately and spontaneously grow when soil and sun and water are offered, so we live by exchange. Tragically, we can refuse and we do. And because we do, we live in a broken world, we dance with hobbled feet and deaf ears. We misstep and collide and lose the patterns. Connectedness becomes confinement and conflict. One refusal makes the next more likely.

And we are on a slow, steady march toward isolation and alienation. Once the dance is halted and the flow broken, the whole circle of life is affected. The health and the integrity of the body (family, community, society) deteriorate and weaken. In theological terms, sin sets in and a series of disasters is set off: mistrust, fear, revenge, hostility, violence, rejection. Another patterning develops, and we adapt to it and move according to its distorted rhythms. We become conditioned to negative responses and destructive behaviors.

What might happen if enemy soldiers, crawling on mined fields, encountered each other suddenly face to face, and one of them extended his hand empty of gun or grenade? Something like this is said to have happened at one human moment during World War I. The conditioning of the other soldier may well mean the vulnerable man is killed. Jesus attempted that kind of disarming and failed. Those who surrounded him, with nails, and orders from on high, were no longer humanly responsive. The pressures of circumstance and role often cause us to make heroes of one another. We have forgotten who we are. We become the extensions of our indifferent and suspicious collective identity.

One of the most unique and attractive features of Jesus' personality was his resistance to that conditioning. John says:"The light shines on in darkness, a darkness that did not overcome it." "Love bent," says J.V. Taylor, "on creating the possibility of an answering love."[3] Love putting rage and cruelty and harshness into a new light, the light of a more complete truth, a more tolerant understanding.[4] Love absorbing evil and so turning it into good. Love proclaiming: No one who comes to me will I ever reject.

Each of us builds our own frameworks for understanding the levels and shapes of love. Charles Williams made a valuable distinction for me in *Seed of Adam*. Mary and Joseph are conversing and Mary says: "Joseph, I am in love." "With whom?" Joseph asks. "No, Joseph," Mary continued, "I am in love."[5] Joseph was not excluded; he was included in a special way. As human beings we love people, individually and uniquely. The scope of our love embraces a small niece, a kindly neighbor, a close friend, an intimate lover, a spiritual guide, a dead parent. We love our planet earth, the people of our world, far and near, our gardens, our books, our church, our hometowns, and even our faithful car. But loving, in all that variety and intensity, is not the same as being in love. The latter is not described by the object to which we relate. It is described by a level of existence, a gift-quality whereby we see and respond to reality from within, with ever-readiness for the possibility of exchange. Falling in love in this sense is something like conversion; it is a metanoia; we are developed from within. Our position changes. We are no longer at the center, an individual seeking completeness. We are immersed in a configuration in which we live and move and have our being. We are integrated into a flow of life that is also our life. Being in love means that no particular object of love, however engaging or passionately regarded, is confused as *the* object. "This also is thou; neither is this thou."[6]

Of course we may think (I do sometimes) that this diminishes the love we bear for someone. But is it diminishing to call a particular love particular when that is its glory? A love affair with life itself is not the same as loving true bits of life. In and through and with our particular loves, we remain in love, open to the mystery and miracle of all that touches us, open to the unknown millions with whom we share space and time, open to the influence of life's experiences and meaning. Thomas Merton perhaps alluded to something like this in his *Asian Journal:* "Love rooted in truth rather than need, love based on no illusions, love that is one with detachment and compassion."[7] I suspect that you and I fall in and out of this level of love. "To love is to die and live again—to live from a new root."[8] Not once, but repeatedly, as we are called and shaped by life's events and by our response-ability. "You are not far from the reign of God," Jesus told the scribe who understood the one great commandment, to be in love.

It is within that framework and that acknowledgment, of the power and beauty of particular love, and the truth and open-endedness of love itself, that I attempt to speak of love and friendship. Never let it be thought that we can be in love without the flesh and blood, the tears and ecstasy, of particular loves. Love can never be abstract. As long as our intense loves do not drown out the melody of life itself, they should be pursued to their fullest potential. Dietrich Bonhoeffer writes: "God wants us to love eternally with our whole hearts—not in such a way as to injure or weaken our earthly love, but to provide a kind of *cantus firmus* to which the other melodies of life provide the counterpoint...where the *cantus firmus* is clear and plain, the counterpoint can be developed to its limits."[9] Love and friendship happen *to* us; being in love happens *in* us. Together they comprise the human adventure.

Often we have heard that the opposite of love is fear. True, with qualification. Perfect love casts out fear. Fear is always fear *of* something. Fear of losing our individuality is the opposite of love. Fear of being penetrated, opened, affected by the force and call of love. Fear of giving up something of ourselves, something vital and irreplaceable, of entering into reciprocity. Beneath every failure to love there is a conviction that it is not safe to give oneself spontaneously to life, to another person, to an object of love. We fear being changed, recreated. Love threatens us. At the end of this fear is hell, complete isolation, loneliness. At the end of love is community, conversion, ongoing transformation.

CARRYING AND BEING CARRIED

"Love is kind...it is not self-seeking." Love is a threshold, an entrance into a life for and from others. It presupposes risk. To love is to be vulnerable. "If you give your heart to no one," C.S. Lewis comments, "it will become unbreakable, impenetrable, irredeemable."[10] The images are physical: breaking and penetrating, hard and soft, stone and flesh, open and closed. Giving your heart to someone ensures it will be broken, pierced, wounded and made malleable. The heart that loves is made of flesh; it is yielding, open to relocating itself. It dares to live for another more than for oneself. It becomes one with the other, in some sense becomes the other. Chardin describes the process as a bursting asunder of the envelope in which our individual microcosms tend to isolate themselves and vegetate.[11] It is the breaking of a membrane, a release from our protective cocoons, a crossing over into the magnetic field of another. It is the end of boundaries and limits and the beginning of a limitless self-pouring and self-transforming. "Truly, what is stiff and hard is a companion of death; what is soft and weak is a companion of life. Therefore, the weapon that is too hard will be broken, the tree that has the hardest wood will be cut down."[12]

We are to love each other as Jesus loved us, laying down our lives as he did. We are to love each other, that is, by acts of substitution. A mother with child illustrates this perfectly. Giving of her time and energy, indeed of her very body and blood, she "carries" the child.[13] We all "carry" those we love, in some way. We carry them by being present to them, by the steady flow of our encouragement and acceptance, by our willing participation in their lives and burdens, by placing ourselves in their place and living their experience with them. We all understand how this "replacement" works: our worry as someone travels, our "vibes" with those in distant places, our desire to remove another's pain, our pride in their success, our joy in their joy.

In a freakish incident with my purse in India, my glasses were stolen. Though I had a second pair, they were not strong enough. I wrote of it to a friend, who happened to be traveling in Australia, herself dependent on glasses. In the past we had on occasion exchanged glasses and discovered that our eyes could adjust to each other's. Yet the most remote thought from my mind at that moment in India was an exchange of glasses. The day she arrived back home from abroad, however, she put her glasses in the mail and they arrived safely. An act of replacement!

What we have not sufficiently explored is the potential of this "substitution" in the case of persons less acceptable to us, or known to us only in the spirit. We need to re-examine the traditional "mystical body" theories and apply in fresh ways what substitution might mean. It is what distinguishes life in and toward God's reign from life outside it. When we can "carry" an "intruder" in our lives, pick up the burdens of someone who is less than a friend, offer them tangibly a bit of our support and understanding, with no conditions attached, then we enter a "mystical" realm.

This living for others is complemented by a living from others. For many of us, love means giving. And all too often, it is self that is at the heart of the giving, our need to give, our choice of what to give, our satisfaction in the results of the giving. Many of us bring food to the meal program at St. Ben's. But a very few invite these same street people to their own homes for a meal. Foreign aid, to be sent to distant lands, is easy to vote for. But what about the foreigners, especially from certain parts of the world, who ask for help within our own borders? Many of us are faithful when friends or family are ill, visiting them, assisting, substituting. But when we are incapacitated, it is more difficult to allow others entrance, to minister to us.

We are to be borne in love, as well as to bear. We are to be given life as well as to extend it to others. Our capacity to receive, to adapt, to be formed and modified by love, is often less developed than our capacity to give. There are grave risks in both. There must be some rhythm of both. It is love's nature to be reciprocal.

PURGING AND PRUNING

"When I was a child I used to talk like a child...when I became an adult I put childish ways aside." Love is not for the immature, the weak-hearted. Love is not a romantic journey, a never-ending series of psychological strokes or spiritual consolations. Those who read the poetry of love, as well as those who write it, will be challenged.

St. Paul's list of the qualities of love (1 Corinthians 13) brings a smile to our lips. It's too much. We are not capable. It is not possible. How surprised I have been to find that description take on concrete names and situations! Not that I have passed the test or completed the course. But I have been given the choice to brood over my injuries and to limit my trust, or to endure love's purging. The language of love is consistent, whether the composer be of an earlier century or contemporaneous. In the lines of those whose wisdom I have sought, I hear echoes of the following: the truth will make you free, after it drags you through humility and vulnerability and trust. Love will make you whole, but only after it dismembers you.

St. Paul reminds us that love will demand of us nakedness and danger, trial and persecution. Jesus tells us simply that it will demand our life. Julian of Norwich comforts us: "God did not say, 'You will never have a rough passage, you will never be overstrained, you will never feel uncomfortable,' but God did say, 'You will never be overcome.'"[14] Gibran's images are severe and shocking. Love crucifies as well as crowns, shakes one's roots as well as caresses one's topmost branches, kneads and sifts the soul, casts it finally into the fire.[15] T.S. Eliot also speaks of fire. It is love who must have devised love's torments. Love wove "an intolerable shirt of flame."[16] Rabindranath Tagore describes love as a sword, flashing like a flame and heavy as thunder.[17] And Bette Midler sings of love as a razor, a hunger, a seed in darkness.[18]

This is not the love of adolescents, of super-stars, of our dreams and fancies. This is the love whereby we embark on a spiritual voyage into the depths of our own egos and selfish waters and onto the mountains of our own integration and conversion. It is the love that beckons us in our human affairs, in our friendships, and our vowed fidelities, the love that lures us into confrontation with the principalities and powers. It is the vocation we pray for, the burden we choose to bear, and the only way we know to find human fulfillment.

Do not try to direct its course, we are advised.[19] We shall not cease from its exploration, assures another, until the "fire and the rose are one."[20] No other decorations will satisfy, says a third, though it hurts as we press it to our bosom.[21] And its blossom will be born after darkness and the cold of winter, sings still another.[22] We read and we meditate and we are moved. And then one day we enter its mystery firsthand, its crowning and its caressing, its hint of fruit, its myriad avenues of explo-

ration. An emptying begins and a pruning. Paradoxes replace
the more facile scripts. We waver in our presumed understanding and grasp of love. We feel the cold winds of hard truths,
the unexpected blows. We wince at the sharp stings and the
dull aches of love's weapons. We fight the flames to no avail.
We are wounded, and we yield to love's demands. Or we live in
eternal regret.

Our encounters with love are individual in size and shape.
Faces loom before your mind's eye and mine, and experiences,
significant, however minor. We recall the moment when we
said, "I am afraid, but yes." Our private stories are adapta-
tions of this poetic paradigm. They range from personal commitments to spiritual experiences, even to love affairs with the
human race. They are yet unfinished and unpredictable. We do
not know the outcomes or the expense. Wherever human beings
are concerned, the exchange can lead to joy or to tragedy. Love is
hidden agony, suspenseful waiting.[23]

DAILY AND DRAMATIC

"If I speak with human tongues and angelic as well, but do not
have love, I am a noisy gong, a clanging cymbal." There is a lot
of noise about love. It is shouted from our billboards and our TV
screens. But romance novels, modern advertising, and soap ope-
ras capture only a few superficial hints. Their gloss and their
shoddiness are only distortions of what transpires in our relationships. Most of us are more familiar with the dailiness of
love than with its rare moments of ecstasy. The demands of
friendship and its dilemmas often outweigh the promised bliss.
A woman was sharing her mourning after the death of a close
friend. "She was difficult to love sometimes," she said. It was
important that even in death the strain and the stress of their
friendship be acknowledged. Few who have loved deeply and
faithfully will deny that the struggle is constant. To accept all
the dimensions of another human life, to adjust, to discover and
continue to discover, to learn and to grow together. To fit two
unique and different personalities in a viable pattern of exchange and to be fruitful in the bargain is perhaps the greatest

of human challenges. and then to bow before the ultimate mystery and inscrutability in that same person, and to accept the distance that will never be bridged.

Simone Weil says: "Friendship is a miracle by which a person consents to view from a certain distance and without coming any nearer, the very being who is necessary to him [or her] as food."[24] Love appreciates the inviolability of the other. Often we learn through numerous errors that we cannot change each other, that we do not own one another. We can only stand at the threshold of another's existence and extend our own gifts, receiving humbly and gratefully the other's offerings. Not comparing, not competing, not bargaining, but offering and receiving. Love works with that exchange and builds what it can. It trusts that other offerings and exchanges will ensue. When the coffer seems empty, love waits. Even when it seems futile, love waits. In human terms this may mean that love atrophies and dies. But better that love die a truthful death than a manipulated relationship be built on shifting sands.

We are "at home" in the presence of love. We are welcomed and accepted whether we have offended, whether we are piebald, whether we have an introverted personality. We can rely on both consolation and criticism. We can stop acting and reveal ourselves, as wretched and worried, as doubting and delinquent. Some years ago my nephew left the priesthood. His mother's pride in her priest-son had been unmistakeable and his decision to leave was a permanent wound. He broke all her sacred images. Yet she welcomed him home, accepted his loss of formal religious practice, rejoiced in his marriage, accompanied him through terminal cancer, and participated in his non-sectarian burial. He was her beloved son.

One of the great wonders of love is its multi-dimensionality. Love uses all the resources available to human beings. It articulates itself through moods, through physical and emotional energies, through the powers of the imagination. The sacredness of a letter. The homeliness of sharing morning tea. The joint rhythms of picking raspberries or baking bread. The poignancy of unintended tears. The routines of leave-taking and reunions. The laughter over foibles. The dreariness of dishes and dirty socks. The restoring nature of simple celebrations. It is as simple as coming home, as regular as breathing, as spectacular as an evening summer sky. It is daily and it is dramatic, familiar and forever a surprise. It is joint word, joint prayer, joint decisions, joint concern, joint agony, joint awe.

Love embodies itself beyond itself, in effective action, in commitments to justice and to creative projects, in political engagement. Love at this level sends people to prison, impels them to substitute their freedom for that of others. A friend of mine wrote from jail: "I believe I am doing what God is asking of me. I hope this jail is a better place because all of us have been here." It converts power into service, obstacles into hope. It finds creative ways to minister and to build community. It manifests itself in both protest and prayer, in sacrifice, in patience, in suffering. Love answers the question: Who is my neighbor? without calculating the risks or consulting the handbook. It is dramatically embodied in a statue erected in Bhopal, India, near the fateful scene of the gas leak in 1984. A mother stands with one hand shielding her eyes, a child in her arm burrowed into her breast, and a second huddled at her knees. It says simply: We want to live.

UNMASKING AND EMPOWERING

"Love does not rejoice in what is wrong but rejoices in the truth." Love reveals the lovers to themselves. Revelations that alter the meaning and course of their life and stretch the very limits of their personality and resources. The range of love's activity, according to Dante, extends from the celestial spaces to the dark abysses of hell.

Love inspires behavior that breaks all the standards and norms for human interaction. From the humorous to the bizarre. From the tiniest details of life to the deepest levels known to humans. Introverts become extroverts, modesty becomes nakedness, defenses become doors by love's recasting and reforming. Peter impulsively leaps into the lake. Francis strips himself, chooses a cave for his trysting place. Catherine de Hueck becomes a "beggar for God." The themes of poetry and drama, love's rare feats and daring sacrifices. The history of the human race: the eruptions and devastations, the soaring and the sordidness of love. The mystery of communion, the ideals and idiosyncrasies of love pledged and love sought, love disrobed and disillusioned. The human adventure!

When one loves, there is a new delight in being alive, new powers of awareness, of perception. Some say, a joyful unreason. Ordinary tasks are elevated; simple events are sacramentalized. Persons are born again, regain an innocence and a purity and a wholeness. They experience physical exhilaration, a propensity for play. One young woman told me her breathing was periodically irregular, as if she were living by new rhythms in a new atmosphere.

New powers sprout, new confidence is gained. Projects are conceived, a community is born, a heritage is transmitted. Love conspires and collaborates and is fruitful. There is a glimpse of self-transcendence, and all that that enables. A capacity for pain, for substitution. An ability to enlarge one's own boundaries. To accept one's hidden scars. To forgive oneself. To learn a new humility.

"Love in action is a harsh and dreadful thing compared to love in dreams."[25] There are hints and sometimes displays of the violence and passion locked up in love's treasury. The totality of love and its all-consuming nature are in conflict with basic human tendencies: jealousy, desire, desperation. Love thwarted and rejected creates the greatest tragedies humans can perpetrate. The illusions of love will eventually be unmasked. Love will be radical in its truth. Innocent and romantic love dies the day we discover that there is some evil in every good, even in the beloved. This gives way to disaster, or to new avenues of exchange.

All of these revelations are the basis for a new experience of sexuality. Our sexuality becomes a sign of our openness to and our oneness with the world about us. It is a basic and primitive experience of the joy of existing, of being in relationship. It provides all the equipment we need to notice and to respond to the beings around us. We are at every moment sexual, and what we ultimately seek is ecstasy, that standing outside of self, in another, a peak experience of human exchange.

Love's revelations are also the basis for a new experience of fidelity. A relationship implies presence, but exchange in relationship points to fidelity. It is the recognition of an ongoing presence, a commitment to the utmost integrity in relating of which one is capable. It leads to creativity and fruitfulness, to ensuring a permanency and continuity of love. Gabriel Marcel says: "In swearing fidelity to a person, I do not know what future awaits us or even, in a sense, what person he [or she] will be tomorrow; the very fact of my not knowing is what gives worth and weight to my promise."[26]

These revelations are likewise the basis for the vows we make, whether we commit ourselves with another human being to a project of human love, or whether we seek to collaborate with God in a project of celibate love. We offer the gift of self, whole and incarnate, with all our resources, placed in trust, our futures to be jointly discerned and determined.

LOVE HAS TEETH

"There is no limit to love's forbearance, to its trust, its hope, its power to endure." Love is dynamic, constantly expanding in meaning. While this seems logical, I find myself surprised by the ever-unfolding and unfurling of love's meaning. A long time ago a friend sent me a card, a lovely "Narnia" street lamp in the foreground, then fertile country, green and full of fascination, comfortable too, and domestic. Beyond, more austere terrain, then distance upon distance to an incredible summit of white magnificence. "We cannot stay at ease," it said, "in the pastures, but we must follow to the 'delectable mountains.'" Once we have seen the flash of snow upon the peak, the climb begins. We enter upon territory ever-widening and more exacting. We are pulled along onto paths more and more precarious.

No one of us is defined by this historical moment. There is always "more" of us, the mystery of us, the bit of the image of God in us. What love meant and asked at one time is no longer true.

We grow and are shaped as love's story develops. "...in every breakthrough to a new level of being, an earlier simplicity, which had its own kind of perfection and beauty, is lost forever. We can, perhaps, think of that love which creates this breakthrough 'suffering' in it, because what has previously expressed love had died in order that the new love may be born."[27]

Love, like life, has cycles and each is valid. "The joy of such a pattern is not only the joy of creation or the joy of participation, it is also the joy of living in the moment."[28] Security in a relationship lies not in its permanency, which is never guaranteed in life, but in the ability to live in the present moment. Love has its seasons and its climates as well. Summers are brief and we pass through winter's freeze before we come upon spring again. Thus we learn the language of love's ascent. Though colored and contoured by each season, love endures and stretches, love is fortified and freed. Love makes impassable passes passable.

Conflict and tension and all the complexities and ambivalences of human beings in action comprise the dialectic of love. Love has teeth, says Helen Luke.[29] It bites, it grips, it tears. It is far from being a gentle, warm emotion. Love resorts to blame as well as blessing. I have often pondered a living parable. A friend and I were skiing in the Jura Mountains. We had taken a common course, but suddenly the ski trails parted in parallel directions. Blowing snow had obscured what might be the through-trail. Hastily we separated, each to explore. By the time I knew I was on the sought-for trail, my friend was knee deep in an impossible route. Should she go back, difficult and time-consuming, or should she try to cross over the gap between us to my trail? She chose the latter route. We lost sight of each other as she descended and maneuvered an incline, an unknown space with possible pitfalls. I, on my side, left the track to try to climb toward her, so she could set her sights. Both of us fell repeatedly and were helpless in our struggles to free ourselves from the soft, deep snow. Eventually she accomplished the feat and arrived on the trail. We were both exhausted, and we somehow each felt the other was responsible for the difficulties we had had. The tension we had felt broke out in blame.

It's an age-old problem. Adam and Eve blamed each other. What might have happened if one of them could have accepted responsibility and they could have approached the consequences united?

Love has the difficult task of balancing freedom and fidelity. For love restricts us, even while it frees us for adventures and fruitfulness we never dreamed of. When is love faithful in putting another's needs and priorities first? And when is love thus bondaged? The discernment of fidelity is a severe test.

Love's meaning unfolds, beyond death itself. I attended a funeral some years ago, the wife of a doctor-friend. Her death from cancer left four small children. A portion of the homily preached that morning lingers in my mind. God would be a betrayer if, after blessing the love of this couple and the love of this family, God said: "It is all a joke. It ends here." Rather, this love, so visible, so wounded, is a sign, a revelation that love must continue, must transcend death. We humans are only part of the mystery of love; we cannot grasp the whole. But the whole is as real as this part.

LOVE CAN DO NO MORE

Love pursues us throughout our lives. We will be caught in its embrace or we will have missed the glory of being human. It schools us for the tasks of love which are demanding: attending to the stranger abandoned on the road, welcoming the prodigal, praying for our enemies, giving witness before courts, forgiving without limit, washing feet, selling all, offering our life as ransom.

The school of love will humble us. We think we have learned love's language and we stumble. We believe we have love in our grasp and we lose it. We are reminded that we are sinful, limited, too small and too weak to bear the beams of love. We weary of love's requests. We resent its endeavor and its expense. We are helpless in its outcome. Love reveals to us our poverty.

The school of love will challenge us. What are we willing to risk, for those we love and those we don't even know? Where will we allow ourselves to be led, in commitment, in mission, in

fidelity? What are we exchanging in this dance, in this network of human exchange? We will be challenged to the limits
of our generosity and self-sacrifice. Love reveals to us the extent
of our riches.

The school of love will give us a degree of wholeness. Time
and eternity are brought together. Flesh and spirit are united.
We are broken and then healed, and the process is repeated until we are a worthy vessel. Would we ever choose not to love, or
to have been loved? We are transformed, at least for moments
and short intervals, into human beings, images of and collabo-
rators with God—whose "arms of love, aching, spent, the world
sustain."[30] Love takes us beyond ourselves, and reveals to us a
glimpse of eternity. Love can do no more. "Now we see indis-
tinctly as in a mirror; then we shall see face to face. There are
in the end three things that last: faith, hope, and love, and the
greatest of these is love." (1 Corinthians 13:12-13)

THREE

COMMUNITY AND CHURCH

"Our morning prayer is a blessing and I so often smile or feel your response as I read and see all the mission-slant in the readings of these days. It is an arid scene here, clergy-dominated, no sense of mission, of outreach, of church for the world. Much of this poverty-stricken church scene is grist to our mill in terms of future work."

A friend and I are living this summer in her cottage in East Anglia. We are a small ecumenical community in the midst of this ecumenical village of Shelfanger. Our neighbors are so in the best sense of that word. Vegetables are exchanged, carpentry repairs are offered, and common concerns are expressed both at the garden fence and at the tea table. In a way not experienced since childhood, I feel part of a basic rural community: mail, milk, and fish delivery, a general store, close neighbors, the vicarage and church, and us. We have some difficulty keeping stray sparrows out of our house, and spiders and beetles roam freely. Our garden is a blend of colored blossoms, fast-growing vegetables, diverse-smelling herbs, and persistent weeds. Just across the road are sugar beets, peas, and wheat. Living in this interdependent setting, one knows something of community and its exchange at its most primitive levels and in its most human manifestations. Community, with its rhythms and regularities, is natural at Shelfanger.

Of course there are death-watch beetles to be feared, as they consume the old timbers that comprise the frames of these cottages. And rain and wind have bashed at times these open fields and unprotected gardens. The man next door lost his wife recently to cancer. My own stay here will come to an end and farewells to my new friends and cottage-refuge will not be easy. All communities experience the pain of their members as well as the fruits of their solidarity.

"All life," says Annie Dillard, "is an interconnected membrane, a weft of linkages like chain mail."[1] All around me nature proclaims that life is interwoven. Some of the hedges have been replaced by new roads, and the retired farmer down the way will tell you of the effects on bird life. We humans can't avoid the imprint of our movements. In our times especially, these movements have world-wide reverberations, sometimes uncontrolled and sometimes uncontrollable.

Chernobyl's effects disturbed us all and made graphic our powerlessness in the face of nuclear power. The sheep in Wales and Scotland were victims of the polluted rain water rushing through the hills and mountains. Milk and fruit are contaminated in some European countries and children will be affected thirty years from now. The long-range damage to Russia itself, to the environment and human life, cannot be calculated.

This is true not only of Russia. A recent series of articles in the United States reveals that America's nuclear weapon industry has unsafely disposed of untold millions of gallons of radioactive wastes. Some of these plutonium-carrying wastes have poisoned ground water. Other wastes have exposed citizens to excessive radioactivity in the air. The "Love Canals" of the U.S. multiply and breed their disastrous consequences. Every nuclear weapon made leaves behind it a trail of litter. Those who are meant to be protected become victims of those very weapons.

The situation in Africa today also illustrates the breakdown of nature's systems. The people are so poor that they over-cultivate and under-fertilize their land. They cut down their trees for fuel because they can't afford more expensive kerosene. They burn animal dung instead of using it as manure. With increasing speed, the top soil blows or is washed away. A desert is left: sand in the Sahel, baked mud in East Africa. Only time and effort can replace the soil cover, and Africans are already borrowing time from nature.

Nature's fragility is evident in our polluted rivers and lakes, in air unsafe to breathe, in the forms of wildlife rendered extinct in recent years, in emergency plans to protect valuable species of plant and fowl. "There is an uncanny resemblance between our behavior toward each other and our behavior toward the earth."[2]

The frailty of the human community is conveyed in news headlines and television documentaries. All the "isms" of our world are an outright denial of community and its inherent quality of exchange. Community has failed when one-eighth to one-fourth of the world's people are hungry. When two billion people do not have safe drinking water. When our minds cannot even comprehend the extent of human suffering and wasted lives. Even the signs commonly posted in our suburbs and city neighborhoods declare this failure: "Beware of vicious dog"— "Children not allowed"—"Keep out"—"Trespassers will be prosecuted." *Danger* is written everywhere, and we have few places where we might escape.

A large block of property owned by a religious order in a midwestern city in the United States is protected at night by a guard with a threatening dog. The gates to the convent warn daytime trespassers and discourage children who might romp in the spacious garden. Somehow the underlying contradictions are not obvious, even to those who follow St. Francis of Assisi.

Despite advances towards unifying and consolidating our global community, we are more than ever an anonymous mass of people, strangers to our neighbors to the south or to the east, and often strangers to the people next door. For many of us, the question: Who is my neighbor? is best not asked. We are embarrassed to read in the newspaper of the death of someone who lives nearby. We are afraid to ask a stranger for help on the highway (or to offer assistance). We feel indifferent to the needs of those who are "different" in any way. Even as Christians we are not all that interested in what happens in the church around the corner from ours or in the ethnic ghettos of our cities. We huddle with a few select friends in our sun parlors, on our golf courses, on our patios, frightened and frozen. We try not to notice what is happening to family farms, to our park lands. And we close our ears to the prophets of a nuclear holocaust or of a revolution in another part of the world. We content ourselves with our dandelion-free lawns and our like-minded congregations. We continue to hope that our health and our bank accounts and our particular political party will hold out. We dread the possibility of the breakdown of our insular, comfortable way of life.

In the midst of this vast failure to find and maintain our common responsibilities, there are flickers of light. Little cells of new life and promise, growing up in unlikely places. People who hold a vision. Tiny incarnations of resistance and struggle and creativity. Base communities, the church of the poor, rising from the ashes of a dying church empire. Little gatherings of searchers and explorers who believe a way can yet be found in the jungle we have allowed to overtake us. These "incarnations" are the subject of this chapter, which explores the importance of: 1) maximizing "moments" of community; 2) developing a consistent community-consciousness; 3) accepting mission as the blessed burden; 4) assuming the costly tasks facing today's emerging church; 5) imposing on ourselves new standards of review, based on mutuality and exchange.

MOMENTS OF COMMUNITY

I always look to St. Ben's in Milwaukee as a community that offers a glimpse of God's realm. Despite its many weaknesses and obvious problems, it is a place where people are known by their first names, where rich and poor, black and white, mingle, and where judgments are not cast nor qualifications needed. People are busy about gospel agendas: feeding the hungry, rescuing the homeless, sheltering the alien, working for peace, upholding women, fostering dialogue, encouraging alternative styles of living.

Two years ago I participated in a small conference in France, with fifteen members of the world community, as diverse as South African, East German, Greek Orthodox, and Argentinian Pentecostal. In the week we lived together and shared our visions, we demonstrated that we relied on each other, even for ongoing encouragement and inspiration. One of that community has since died, and most of us have not been in actual contact since. Yet I dare to say that we remain a community, in intention and in deed.

Some would say that the nature of community is to bring together and bind together those who would otherwise have little in common. Crises, natural disasters, accidents, tragedies of all sorts, seem to bear this out. I remember a night spent in the basement of an apartment building during a tornado watch. I saw some of my neighbors up close for the first time. We sat huddled together, telling stories, quieting the children, and learning our community history. A hostage situation in Iran, a volcanic eruption in the Cameroons, a mudslide in Colombia, a child lost anywhere in the world, all call forth the instinct for community.

Our sisters in India live an hour's jeep ride from Bhopal and yet, at the time of that disaster, people streamed into their compound. One moving story relates the efforts of some of the women, grieving themselves, to relieve the physical distress, if not the anguish, of a young mother who had lost her nursing baby.

Why is it that we can rediscover the communitarian nature of our life when life is in jeopardy? And then we go our individual ways when conditions ease, withdrawing from the give and take, rebuilding our walls of apathy and remarking our restricted zones. We are ashamed to be human, it would seem, until we are threatened, and then we form community as quickly as frightened children approach any available stranger.

I have been a member of a religious community for over thirty years. It should be long enough to teach anyone the value and the strength of shared life. And yet, many of us, myself included, have not only failed to find and build community, we have failed to believe in its potential. Community, when it works and even when it does not, is something pressingly real—persons in a single space and time, meeting and interacting, rubbing shoulders and exchanging dreams, touching and embracing, learning to walk in some harmony, exploring the ways in which we free and freeze one another. I see more clearly the ambiguities in our life. Despite this, many sisters choose to live alone, to resent the energies needed to make a community operative. Some feel alienation in our anonymity, in the inevitable bureaucratic tangles, in hesitant identification with those who are conservative or authoritarian. How can one feel bonds with a community of 1800? I myself have often felt isolated, and even in exile. Hypocritical also, professing to be Franciscan and living very middle-class. Claiming to be a person of compassion and walking away from so many blatant needs.

On the other hand, I see a tremendous potential for us as a congregation. Situated in more than ten countries, we can model something our world desperately needs: a community united across cultures, bridging first and third worlds, offering each other the unique gifts of our native lands, being shaped and challenged by our differences.

Perhaps we take the word "community" too literally, and too narrowly. Martin Buber says that community is where it happens and that is where it should be celebrated.[3] We stand in a reciprocal relationship with one another, but we all stand as well in a reciprocal relationship with a single living center. That center is what we have in common, even when all else seems flimsy. A community is not a static entity. It is an event unfolding, depending on the faith and efforts of all involved. I find that I am more alert—because of process philosophy, because of Gandhi, Thomas Merton, the liberation theologians, because of Nelle Morton, Rosemary Haughton, Dorothy Soelle—to experiences of community in both familiar and unexpected places. I recognize community in a common life with my sisters, in places like Shelfanger, in small mission outposts in India, at peace demonstrations or political rallies, at worship, at ecumenical conferences. The important thing is to become a living member of each potential community, even when it lasts but a day or a week.

A Methodist minister and I once spent a week in a small inner-city church, fasting and praying for peace, and gathering around us during various hours of the day a motley, searching stream of people. It is one of my most vivid memories of a living, throbbing, community. Contacts with sisters in Germany, Guatemala, and India have given me a network, a sisterhood that enriches me with Spanish music, German art, and Indian dance. Having friends and potential homes in places like South Korea, or Australia, or Egypt, or Colorado makes the world much more a family than a mass of faces and statistics. This summer I climbed a mountain in Scotland with two friends. As the going got rougher, and the gale winds threatened to blow us off Ben Lawers, I knew how physical community can be and how necessary are the reassuring grasps and the protective closeness of companions.

It would be naive to assert that community can be achieved by physical proximity alone. Institutional life often has little in common with community. Too many marriages and family groupings testify that more than a shared roof and bank account are required. Too many convents and monasteries betray the way of life that they are intended to portray. And as a result, community becomes one of those realities that has all but lost its meaning. Even the addition of words such as base, peace, resistance, or ecumenical, cannot quite resurrect the vitality and promise of the hoped-for reality. It is said that in Tanzania one does not use a person's name or ask it until the holder has offered it.[4] Perhaps those of us who live in community should stop claiming it, and allow others to decide when we deserve it. When our life is "with unity," when our outreach and our internal harmony are a distinguishing mark, when we have a distinct relationship with a distinct center, the term will once again come to life.

CONSPIRING TOGETHER

"If you live alone, whose feet will you wash?" Attributed to St. Basil, the question suggests that something fundamental is lacking in a solitary life. There is a longing in every human being to be known, to be deemed worthwhile. Without the possibility of exchange, our very being as persons is threatened. Life in solitude, if it persists, often has disintegrating effects. Complete and total isolation is the highest form of punishment, as our prison systems affirm.We die for lack of meaning, which is lack of relationship. We need one another to know who we are. Our life in common gives us a history and a future. Vincent Donovan tells of an experience with a group of high school students. He asked one girl "If something important happened to you, who would be affected?" "You mean if I committed suicide or something?" she asked. He accepted her morbid example. Without any further thinking she replied: "Mary here, and my mother." No one in the room protested. In fact, they agreed. Donovan concluded that if this young woman were typical, America's greatest need was to find again a sense of community.[5]

We exist in relation to others. And yet we continue, it seems, to place our individual existence and fulfillment over against the truth of community. We develop the organizational dimension of our lives at the cost of its inner cohesiveness. In my own religious order we have long struggled with the tension between personal and corporate demands. For so long in our history individual priorities and gifts were subordinated to the needs of the whole congregation. More recently we have given great latitude to personal choice. Sometimes it seems that the community now has no right to expect or suggest or require anything of its members. We continue to seek the balance between personal integrity and a faithful spirit of community.

So many of the homilies offered in our churches, so much of the literature adorning our church racks, tout personal piety as the surest and most blessed way to sanctity. These imply that a sense of social responsibility and political engagement are the charisms of a few or are optional activities for those with the time and tendency. We still think in terms of individual vocations and individual conversions. We don't see ourselves as a united community, acknowledging our need of each other's gifts and committed to a common vision. We count heads and we confuse our different functions with our common priesthood. Our penchant for organization leads to the plethora of meetings and committees that fill our lives, from national associations to local chapters, from annotated reports to conference resolutions. How many of us are approached only through our secretaries? How long can we function sanely without benefit of a pocket calendar? Whom do we dare visit without an appointment? Many of us are simply too busy to build community, or too important in our own eyes to adapt to a communal and hospitable way of life.

Community begins in a vision that brings people together and binds them in one hope. It grows as the members conspire together on behalf of love and justice and freedom. Community is a sign that it is possible to live on a human scale, even in our world of GNPs, megaton bombs, and mammoth-size poverty pockets. It is a place where we learn to live at the pace of people and of nature rather than speedways and computers. Community is concerned with bread, with literacy, with civil liberties, with peace. I know that Rosemary Haughton has said it formally, but many of us share a belief that caring people wherever they are constitute community, constitute indeed the church.[6] More and more we affirm that the only relevant church is that which is open and inclusive and committed to defending life or improving it. The church as an empire or as a depository of truth or as a claim to status does not interest many of us. We accept the remains of its authority only when something is stirring inside it, when we see the creative testimony of men and women struck by the gospel. When the gospel is re-enacted in today's Galilees and Samarias. When people know the gospel "by heart," whether they be church functionaries or ordinary people with a purpose, church-goers or simple seekers.

It is this sense of identity and community that characterizes the spirituality we hunger for. This is the ecumenical movement, a movement towards unity, not church unity per se, but human community. A movement that values each human community and seeks to promote mutual exchange. A movement that maximizes the resources of every region and redistributes them according to need. It is along the path of spirituality, of a living response to the gospel, that unity will emerge. As we walk that path together, we will be compelled to draw out the implications for all our relations with one another.

Recently I spent a week at a small monastery in the mountains of Bosnia in Yugoslavia. In a search for an ecumenical spirituality, we crossed the barriers of East and West, of diverse denominations and traditions. We were a place of paradox. An Orthodox monastery located at one of the celebrated sites of partisan resistance in World War II. Cloistered Coptic sisters mingling with post-Vatican II religious. The poverty of the Yugoslavian countryside contrasting with the material and spiritual treasures of an ancient religious tradition. We bore in our beings the poles of alienation and of unity. Spirituality spoke to us of the wholeness of the Christian life and of the interpenetrating of our lives. At the heart of it all is the call to live in exchange, to reject no one who comes to us. Saints are not sectarians. Saints are signs of the oneness of the human condition.

Perhaps God is not as interested as we think in our practice of religion.[7] Perhaps God is, as the God of Isaiah was, interested in *life*. "What care I for the number of your sacrifices?...New moon and sabbath, calling of assemblies...these I cannot bear...though you pray the more, I will not listen...make justice your aim; redress the wronged, hear the orphan's plea, defend the widow." (Isaiah 1:11-17) Our personal faith and personal relationship to God are inadequate. We come together as community to remember who we are. We worship together for the same reason. Our faith is justified only when we make visible our covenant with God and with God's people.

The Old Testament spoke: Do unto others as you would have them do unto you. This was a mandate to live in relationship, justly and independently. In the New Testament Jesus instructs: what I just did was to give you an example; as I have done, so you must do. Don't use your own sense of justice and fairness as your criterion. Rather, my example is the criterion for your interaction with others. It is a new vision, a new kind of formation. Jesus washed the feet of his own small community and bade them to wash one another's feet. It is the special characteristic mark of the Christian, the washing of feet. John's gospel actually leaves us with that message as Jesus' memorial. It is the "other side" of the Eucharistic meal.

For three years, Jesus had prepared his disciples for their mission. But only now, at the end, did he offer them this memorial, the Eucharist. He wanted them to understand its grave significance. A significance made even more clear in the days that followed. They were to have no doubts about the relationship between bread broken and wine poured out, and the sacrifices to be demanded of Jesus' followers. The Eucharist and the willingness to serve, to suffer and die for others, are one act. Everything in the gospels leads up to that solemn parting event: do this in memory of me. These rites—breaking bread, washing feet—are symbols of the rite performed publicly on Golgotha.

In the act of eating together (com-pan-ioning) we become a community. But the true test of our unity is the service we offer daily and indiscriminately. For a Christian community, breaking bread and service are one complete act; thus the scandal of Christians refusing to share bread at a common table, of Christians regularly accepting the rite without any real commitment to be transformed themselves and to participate in the transformation of their surrounding world.

We are forced to ask ourselves: Have we embarked upon a new mode of life, or have we joined another club? Which is more easily identifiable, the diversity of ministries within my community, or our Franciscan charism? Is the Eucharistic food for me as an individual with my private needs, or is it also food for the building up of the body which is all of us? Is the Eucharist a rite for those properly initiated and enrolled, or is it the visible bond of a broken and sinful community?

Can we develop a community-consciousness? Not one that denies the individual or refuses the benefits of organization; but one with a sense of our relatedness, with a common identity and a common responsibility. A habit of thinking and acting that leads to an identity larger than ourselves. A kind of listening ability that makes us accessible and vulnerable to one another. A lifestyle that accepts rather than inflicts suffering. A sense of self that is incomplete without the community to which we belong. A sense of priorities and decision making that considers all, and leans toward those with the greatest needs.

IMAGES OF AN EMERGING CHURCH

Rosemary Haughton says: "A community which works, studies, and prays together in order to serve some ultimate good— which is God, whatever image they happen to be using—is a church in embryo, though it can only truly be called 'church' when it has reached the point of being able to articulate its own meaning as in some way Christ-centered."[8]

We are witnesses today to the development of many such communities: family groups, students, social activists, prayer groups, groups in prison, groups of married and celibate together. Some come together for a specific purpose, others take on a long-term service, others are developing according to circumstances and events. All are searching for a way to make sense of their lives, to be participants in the shaping of their futures, to find the dynamic that links them to other seekers of justice and truth. "This means that if anyone is in Christ, he [she] is a new creation. The old order has passed away; now all is new." (2 Corinthians 5:17)

As these communities take shape, a certain style becomes evident. As members, each confronts his or her willingness to be broken, like the Winnie Mandelas of South Africa, the fence-cutters of Great Britain, those who witness for peace in Nicaragua. Our pain will be a common pain, including the fear and frustration of the Lebanese, the poverty of the Appalachians, and the disenfranchisement of the laity in our churches. We will learn to integrate our own woundedness. Acknowledge our privileged (and deprived) middle-class existence. Confess our weakness in the face of seductive careers. Accept the bruises and scars of broken relationships, unsuccessful marriages, unrealized dreams.

We must become willing to let go of the obstacles that hinder these emerging communities: our personal pride and ambition, our illusions about ourselves. No one of us is the perfect candidate for community. Each of us has an enlarged capacity for selfishness and self-deceit. Can we allow it to shrink, to make room for plurality and for communion? Will we allow bits of our egos to be shattered so that a common sense of discernment may develop? Can we learn to give without calculating the losses and to receive without shame? Surely, this is why we enter novitiates and accept missionary training. This is the goal of ongoing formation and ecumenical education. This is the underlying reason for joining with others in a common venture of faith.

We must possess a willingness and an ability to be alone. For paradoxically, it is from our solitudes that we speak and act effectively. Our truest words are born in silence. Our inner resources become the gift we lay at the feet of community. Only in recovering our deepest selves can we communicate freedom and wholeness to others. Can you not name the silent, strong teachers who have left traces on your soul as you journeyed? A dying man in Norwich whose wisdom and experience we sought this summer. My mother whose teachings have continued to feed my spirit these thirty-five years since her death. An elderly woman who shows the way by her own divesting and her spirit of adventure.

We will begin to spawn a community that has no distinct boundaries and no strict agendas. We will be busy about removing our own prejudices rather than debating rules for membership. We will attract and invite the most diverse of God's people. The least among us will lead us in new styles of leadership and service. We will be less sure about our truth and its practice, eager to adapt to a new moment and a new insight. We will make mistakes and rally ourselves to learn from them.

In our ministry we will strive to be equals. In our prayer we will be one. In our poverty of spirit we will be rivals. In our Eucharistic celebrations, we will most be community, refusing no one, serving one another, finding nourishment for today's common burdens and hope for tomorrow's common crises. We will be

the body of Christ, not metaphorically, but members one of another, conscious that any dis-union is dismemberment. We will
become a new church, discovering our counterparts in other parts
of the world, united in a common mission.

For this emerging church is above all a church in mission.
"Go forth and bear fruit, fruit that will endure...that the world
may believe that I sent you." Not building up little kingdoms,
to pad individual pride. Not competing for credit for honest
work and willing overtime. Not clinging to successes, and being
burdened by failures and disappointments. But sowing the seeds
in a given moment and place so that justice and hope might take
root. Practicing agape towards one another and doing good even
to those who persecute. Reducing the weight borne by those
who lead and those who suffer. Learning to become the one
bread and the one cup that assuages the real hungers and
thirsts of our world.

There is but one mission. We are linked to one another as
places of exchange. There are no private corners to take refuge
in, to protect us from the cries and curses of suffering human beings. There are no free countries as long as militarism and ter-
rorism claim the lives of innocent victims. There are no
antiseptic places exempt from the grime and grief of unhealthy
factories and unsafe city streets. There are no groups that have
"made it" as long as unemployment and homelessness haunt the
land. There are no growing churches as long as we are divided
and discriminating. There is no security as long as our children
face a threatening future. There is no peace possible until we
learn to abolish the causes of war from our own hearts.

There is a common need and a common responsibility. There
is strength in solidarity and hope in creative explorations.
There are bridges being built and ambassadors of reconciliation
afoot. There is new partnership in suffering. There are voices of
conscience echoing around the globe. There are new communities
rising up: of physicians and scientists, of Buddhists and Men-
nonites, of tax resisters, of women, of lay ministers, and of converted clergy. It will be difficult for today's missionaries to
count converts and to delineate territories. It will be more im-

portant to join resources with all those willing, and to find the connections that heal and unite.

The credibility of this emerging church will not stem from claims to authority or orthodoxy, nor from balanced budgets or skills in administration. Neither will it come from theological expertise or political neutrality. Its credibility will be its obedience to a single mandate: Remember me. It will be shown by a downwardly mobile life style, a willingness to take risks; by sincere and humble service, by friendship with the marginalized and the anguished. Theology will derive from discipleship. Teaching will come from the living scripture text, contemporary history, and from those adversely affected by it. The priority will be to accompany the people of God on the move.

TODAY'S TASKS

It is the task of this church to liberate its members from the need to control and from the need to be controlled. Believing in our own ability to create change, rather than relying on the actions of the influential. Not pretending and playing roles, kowtowing to those who make decisions for us, and exempting ourselves from careful discernment and choice. Free to accept others with all their awkwardnesses, taking everyone's opinion into account. The powers of this world, in both church and society, are more and more discredited. Jesus' position on the cross seems like a strange way to lead a people, but it is a new kind of power. A power that is willing to bear pain for the sake of the truth and as a means of achieving peace. A power that continues to make its point even as it suffers defeat. That makes itself accessible to a greater power to work in and through it.

It is the task of this church to name the sins of society, to demand basic rights for those forgotten or virtually eliminated. The gods of a nation are not our god. National security, unlimited pursuit of prosperity at others' expense, race or class ideologies, are idols. It is a sin to build weapons, in the name of deterrence or any other name. It is a sin to threaten aggression, to substitute force for persistent negotiation. It is a sin to condemn others for the evils we ourselves perpetrate. Having called the idols by name, we are called to conspire against them, to repent and convert, and to free ourselves from our complicity with them.

It is the task of this church to search out complicated issues and discover the connections between micro- and macrocosm. To become communicators and interpreters for those who rely on mass media. To interpret public issues in the context of scripture and to combine prophecy and protest, no matter the scorn and ostracism. Apartheid is not just a South African problem. It is the problem of all who live ignorant of the implications of their lifestyles and choices. Whose oranges and bananas are these in our supermarkets? The fruit at the cheapest rate may well be expensive for those who picked it in Honduras or South Africa. The gospel does not permit us to live as tourists, shirking responsibility for the country in which we live, indifferent to the effects of our actions and the cost of our comforts.

Lesslie Newbigin says that "Jesus' life, ministry, death, and resurrection have made such an impact on the human situation that henceforth every human culture is called into question."[9] The conversion needed is that we begin to understand history and to assess the world's agenda within the framework of our faith. Most of us have been convinced that what concerns our public life is subject to an altogether different set of principles, those of secular science or secular politics. Religion over the centuries has become an experience that is personal and private. The values involved don't apply to the larger, more public, world. That world is one of facts; religion is a matter of personal opinion.[10]

It is the task of the church to pierce this dichotomy and to close the fissure between private and public. Christians can't accept that there are areas of human life not subject to the gospel. That there are human authorities and institutions which are independent of the judgments of scripture. That there are levels of creation that have no ultimate purpose and for which there are no final norms. The Christian will not allow idols to replace the God of all life. Rather, the community must struggle to make viable the best alternative among available political entities. It must broaden its understanding of ecumenism. It must be part of the search for a witness that is more coherent and more credible to the whole human community. Finally, the community relies on the various cultures of the world, on the world community, to enlarge its understanding of scripture, of all scriptures, to correct its limited vision, and to help shape its priorities in mission.

INTERSECTING CIRCLES
How close are your circles and mine to participating in the launching of this new church? What clues do we have, as we look at our own small (or large) communities, struggling to be faithful, discouraged at times, daring to hope that we resemble the "body" and are building it up?

I ask myself, and I invite you to ask the following questions: What is sacred in our community? Is it the life and gifts of each member? Is it the life around us, fragile, weak, tentative? Do we know the holiness of ordinary things: the evening primrose, the newborn deer, the heather on the hills, the music of the wind, our momentary encounters with strangers, the tenderness of touch? Are our prayer and worship creation-centered? What do we honor: fidelity and honesty, gratefulness and creativity? What do we celebrate: the seasons, human rites of passage, reconciliations, our interdependence?

How and where are we formed? By the scriptures, and a common longing that they shed light on contemporary events? By the wisdom and experience of those who have been wounded by the gospel? By wilderness experiences, voluntary displacements, vulnerability in trusting and loving? By times of bewilderment and fear and tragedy? With whom do we seek companionship for our journey: the *anawim*, the weaker peoples of our earth? With peasants and poets, learners, the unfit, the mystics and radicals, with global citizens?

What belongs to us? Are we mobile, temporary, rather than permanent builders, part of a movement rather than an empire? Do we claim responsibility for our church, our native land, the earth and its gifts? Are the peoples of different tongues our brothers and sisters? Are the deserts and woodlands and lakes part of our concern? Are we capable of a relationship as big as the universe? Are we influenced by the truth and wisdom and beauty of world religions? Do we cherish and appreciate the cultures that cross our path? Are we compassionate toward ourselves, our energies, our personal needs? Do we own our feelings and our prejudices? Are we willing to surrender what blocks the channels of life between ourselves and other human beings, between our image of self and our true selves? Are our circles constantly expanding and intersecting?

What meaning do we have for those we meet? Are we a blessing? Do we invest something of ourselves? Is our power one of encouraging hope? Do we mend creation and lift human burdens? Are we patient with darkness and mystery and the metanoia of others? Is our word whole with our life? Or are we a curse? Are we unable to trust, to lose control? Do we cling to our collected goods and to our illusions? Are we bored with life, paralyzed with fear and guilt? Are we careless about life, pessimistic about human potential? Are we quick at criticism and judgment, and slow at self-reflection and self-sacrifice?

In India, when people meet or part they often say *Namaste.* This means: I honor the place in you where the whole universe resides. I honor the place in you that contains love, light, truth, peace. When you are in that place in you, and I am in that place in me, there is only one of us.[11] It is that awareness that we seek, that commingling of the personal and the public, of the local and the universal.

Pat Pechauer sought that truth, and gave up her life as she hurried to a prayer service after the United States bombing of Libya. Helen Stotzer-Kloo believed in that journey, and died after a mission to Jerusalem with Protestant and Roman Catholic pilgrims. JoAnn Brdecka understood that language, and succumbed to cancer only after she had broken through ecumenical and sexist barriers. Others are in prison because they seek that vision. Others are exiled, refugeed, living in fear of torture and death. Friends of all of us share the lot of outcasts and the lepers of our society because they believe a community such as I have described is possible. In the time I am given I want to honor their witness and their sacrifice by my small efforts to create such a church. "For I have given you an example, that you also should do as I have done." (John 13:15)

FOUR

FORGIVENESS AND CONVERSION

"We know something about all this terrain: snowy peaks, slippery crags, scree, rock, verdant grass and glorious alpine flowers. I am sorry for all the wounds and hurt and pain. I would not have chosen this route if I had known and I am looking for a way which is least damaging. . . .I can only say I'm sorry and I love you."

An apt image for the demands of forgiveness and repentance; a joint climb up a dangerous mountain. Into the unknown, across precipices, along threatening terrain, with uncertain steps. Tested every inch of the way. A fear of falling and a fear of losing one's companion. Tension in every muscle. Terror in one's heart. Could all be lost? It is as unthinkable to go back as it is to continue. A decision must be made. We both want to go on exploring, learning, discovering new visions and vistas. Therefore you and I must forgive. And you and I must repent.

It was much harder than I realized, being repentant myself and offering another forgiveness. And perhaps I knew why. Most of my experiences of forgiveness entailed persons whom I related to more casually, whose relatedness, though vital, was not so intimate that I could not endure some breakage. And most of my experiences of repentance entailed bits of myself and of my life that I could give up without any damage to my very

61

core, to my central system of beliefs. This was different! This was terribly personal and terribly costly!

Repentance, says Helen Luke, means the abandonment of all self-pitying guilt feelings in order that we may turn and face the dark truth.[1] And pardon, says Charles Williams, is a re-identification of love.[2] Both require a largeness of spirit, a generosity that we cannot always muster. Both require a passion for something that transcends ego and self-image, and that thrusts us into the pain of self-revelation and self-knowledge, into the purifying fires of unselfish love.

I am not speaking, mind you, of life's daily thorns and adjustments: you neglected to remember my anniversary of beginning this job, I failed to mention the part you had played in the planning of the meeting. Hurt feelings, missed moments, slights in our daily rounds of affection, mutual understanding, and acceptance are also grounds for repentance and forgiveness. But here I speak of the crisis moments in our lives when we are not at all sure we can repent or forgive, those critical places where everything we seem to stand for comes in conflict with the demands placed on us by someone we genuinely love and respect. These experiences test our love to determine whether it is something we hold in trust and which holds us as do the elements about us; or whether it is merely something we hold to ourselves, stubbornly and blindly.

The exchange inherent in forgiveness is one of the strongest motifs of the gospels and hence of Jesus' continuing presence among us. In this chapter I intend to examine the dynamics of forgiveness and repentance from the following approaches: 1) the demands of forgiveness; 2) the demands of integrity; and 3) the key to the defeat of evil.

THE DEMANDS OF FORGIVENESS

In those crisis moments, which are also kairos moments, the demands of forgiveness and conversion are revealed. We read the scriptures too glibly. "Seventy times seven" trips off our tongues. Of course we don't understand that that means 490 bowings of our ego, 490 surrenderings of our self-will and our self-righteousness. And actually, it doesn't mean that. It means there must be no limit to our forgiveness, no matter the size or the number of wrongs inflicted on us. Life and love can only continue to flow and transform us if we forgive. The seeds of love must be eternally resown. And forgiveness is that re-identification of love—love revisited, love replanted, love recovered and renamed.

In our celebration of reconciliation rites and communion services, we often forget the actual scriptural injunction: leave your gift at the altar, go first to be reconciled with your brother or sister and then come and offer your gift. I recall a poignant tale told by a father, who was also a Presbyterian minister. He had recently baptized his grandson. He shared the profound joy that he had experienced as he and his daughter received communion on that occasion. It was the first time they had broken the Bread of the Eucharist together in several years. Then he recounted how the two of them had had an intense fallout which reached a climax at a church celebration. His daughter had felt forced to attend because of family image. They stood rigidly side by side. When the moment of communion came, she suddenly bolted from the church, unable to approach the table with her father. He also left the church and pursued her, to no avail. The baptism of her son was the scene of their complete reconciliation, and the two were able to receive once again the broken particles and experience wholeness.

In our liturgies the sign of peace sacramentalizes that scriptural mandate. How important it is that we extend our heart as well as our hand to those who worship with us! At all our Eucharistic meals we preface the sharing of bread and wine with a communal prayer, a family prayer: forgive us our sins as we have forgiven those who sin against us. We recognize, implicitly at least, that there is no eucharist, no sacred meal, no exchange of life, unless we are in truth a reconciled community. Awesome is our responsibility as families, as segments of our local congregations, to authenticate our action with our mutual repentance and conversion!

Not only are we required to forgive those near and dear to

us, we are commanded to forgive those who strike us, those who rob us, those who take advantage of us. We are commanded to love our enemies and to pray for our persecutors, in the manner of Stephen at his stoning, in the manner of Edith Stein, victim of Auschwitz. As did Pope John Paul II when he visited his would-be assassin in prison. In the manner of the demonstrators at Williams International, who were later arrested, but who offered handshakes of peace to the company's representatives and to the local police. Like the young husband and father in Milwaukee who publicly forgave the murderer of his wife and child. Like Jesus who fulfilled the heavy demand: Father, forgive them. They know not what they do. And sealed his words with his death on the cross.

We might well ask why we are required to bestow forgiveness without measure, and without regard to worthiness. Is there not something inhuman about it all? Precisely. Forgiveness is an act whereby we enter into the realm of divine action. We behave as sons and daughters of a merciful God in whose image we are fashioned. We place ourselves where we hope to be for all eternity, in the position of accepting and identifying with all those for whom Jesus suffered and died. We choose companionship with all those whose association we will have in the new realm of God. However difficult it is for our human pride, we say as much: Jesus forgave all. Jesus offered reconciliation and forgiveness. I must do no less.

Having said that, we recognize the human consequences of this "divine" intent. For our gift of forgiveness to be authentic, it must represent the end of blaming, of projecting, of self-defending. It must be rooted in true humility, in the recognition of our own humanness and our own failures. Without these elements of humility and a genuine acceptance of the other without recrimination, our forgiveness will be shallow and superficial. Have you not also on occasion said: I forgive you, but do you realize how deeply you have wounded me, how undeserved your blow was? I forgive you, but you are really the sinner in this, you understand. I would never be guilty of your sin. I condescend to pardon you. I forgive you, but I will remind you often in the future that you have seriously offended me. I won't let you forget my goodness and my remittance of your guilt. Or, if we don't say all that, we find subtler ways to convey the same messages.

My belief is that we must stay with our own human situation, acknowledge the limitations of our understanding, especially of the other's motives, and recognize the contributing causes we bring to this conflict. Above all, we must realize our own potential for wounding and inflicting pain on others, even on those whom we love.

In the deepest throes of my own woundedness, I know that there has to be a moment when I simply surrender. I don't understand. I am bleeding. I can't accept the rationale or the action. I feel the pain of the blow. But I also love the other person, and I do not want to continue to block the life we exchange. I do not want to lose or break the bond that has united us. I value that more than I regret and lament the injury. I can no longer cling to that final illusion that the one I love is without human weakness. "We would rather be ruined than changed. We would rather die in our dread than climb the cross of the moment and let our illusions die."[3] I can no longer view the injury as the supremely significant action of the one I love. And I cannot blame life or my friend for not satisfying the hunger in me that life be perfect and relationships inviolable. Forgiving is love persisting though it is injured, dismayed, and mystified. It is love keeping open the borders.

At that moment I choose to forgive, to try to forgive. And I can only do that when I bring my reality into meditative prayer. When I sit quietly in the presence of the pain and the love, the conflict and the call, when I allow the anguish to rip me apart while I hold the other person in open and loving hands. That struggle may be protracted and repeated, and it may never completely subside. By embracing the journey onward, I begin the slow process of catching up, in my feelings and my memories, with the vision I have of a relationship rooted in and built on love. I become forgiving even while my being resists, before my head and heart agree on the implications. Jonathan Graham speaks for all of us in *He Came unto His Own:*"He who first made the breath-taking discovery that at the heart of the universe is love...learned this secret not...from the experience of a pure and faithful married love. He learned it from the breaking of his own heart."[4] Each of us comes by way of pierced and shattered hearts to the love that spills itself out in forgiveness.

Repentance is equally difficult. In fact, it may demand more humility than does forgiveness. It is often easier to absolve than to ask for mercy. The more"equal" the relationship, the greater the challenge. And what about begging forgiveness of those "smaller" than us? I remember a time when I displayed anger, irritation at least, to a beloved niece. She had accidentally dropped ice cream on the carpet. I was tired and crabby. I snapped at her and immediately her smile turned to hurt and fear. I should have asked her to forgive me my quick emotion and my misplaced priorities. We are, most of us, very adept at justifying our behavior and condoning our stubborn fixations: I did nothing wrong! Repentance asks of us an unbending, a letting go of our immaculate self-images, an admission of weakness and sin.

We know the cost of this dynamic in our closest human relationships. We experience the damage that is done when forgiveness is withheld or when repentance is not forthcoming. How quickly the threads weaken and the tapestry deteriorates! How fast trust diminishes and suspicion crowds into the relationship! How difficult, then, to touch the wound and to believe in its eventual healing! What are the ramifications and the side effects in relationships that are far less personal and far more complicated? What is the erosion and the harm when the conflict is between groups in society or between nations? What do repentance and forgiveness mean in our world of increasing armaments and cold war tensions? In our world of anonymous and faceless predators? Can we expect that there will be a touch of the divine in the cuthroat, ruthless world of global powers and conflicting ideologies? Is it not naive, even blasphemous, to speak of repentance and forgiveness in that context?

Most of us were attentive spectators of the several summit meetings between Mikail Gorbachaev and Ronald Reagan. Could any of us in our wildest dreams imagine that one of these central figures on this world-stage would ask the other's forgiveness? For persistent mistrust, for consistent efforts to deceive, for labels inflicted and judgments passed? And yet, as we followed their entourages to Geneva, Reykjavik, and Washington isn't that exactly what we had to hope? That a bit of humanity would show through the diplomacy and the guardedness and the protocol, and open the way to human relatedness? One important degree of assurance the meetings did offer is due to the fact that Reagan and Gorbachaev met face to face, shook hands, and looked each other in the eye. They were persons together. And that is the key to the process of reconciliation.

We succeed as nations and as armies to perpetuate the enemy-image as long as the enemy is faceless. No one dropping the atom bomb on Hiroshima saw the faces of the victims. The secret of the relentless bombings in Vietnam, Laos, and Cambodia was their facelessness. The bombs hit targets, anonymous targets, not people. Once we sit in the same room as our enemy and speak to one another as human beings, something of the enemy-barrier is necessarily punctured. Would Arab and Israeli hate each other so much if they knew each other's names and family histories? Would brothers in Central America seek to kill one another if they first shared their rations and swapped photos of their children?

Names are important. What a difference it makes in correcting and redeeming history when Japanese and United States traditions are shared, when the Russian soul is mirrored in the gentle face of a conference participant, when we see Daniel Ortega shaking the hand of the pardoned prisoner, Hasenfuss.

Prisoners have names, and so do wardens. The protester who refuses to unblock an entrance has a name and a history. So does the policeman ordered to make the arrest. The man or woman living on the streets, scrounging for food and embarrassing the downtown merchants, has a name and a story. So do those who refuse them help or those who operate shelters or do social work. The welfare victim is not a case, but a human being with a lot of misfortune in his or her background. The obstinate senator may be a dyed-in-the-wool Republican, but he or she is also a husband and a father. So much of the alienation in our world is based on restrictive labels and self-convincing stereotypes: rude young people, lazy unemployed, neglectful mothers, greedy businessmen.

How do we lead our society back to honoring faces and names and stories, away from escape into statistics and labels and case loads? Our size and our complexity complicate this effort. But each time that "enemies" face each other and use one another's proper name, a breakthrough occurs. A realization at least that this is another human being in his or her own set of circumstances. A single small door opens to the possibility of mutual acknowledgment and mutual understanding. Forgiveness for an offense to one's property or person, or for large-scale destructive acts, depends on a personalization of the victims and the offenders. Repentance as well requires that victims and targets become human like oneself.

Yes, this is a dream, and we have moved too far in the opposite direction. We live consistently amid "sides," amid opposing and hostile forces. Life cannot flow or heal or mature. Similar barricades exist in our individual lives and in our church communities. We have not yet invited that conservative bishop or that fundamentalist pastor to sit down with us and chat. We have not yet given our difficult supervisor or our offending neighbor the benefit of a personal call. Perhaps we have not yet forgiven from our hearts the person we love most. Instead we have retreated, closed certain doors, and declared a kind of stalemate. The love is blocked and life begins to atrophy. It is time to apply the doctrine of atonement to all our human relationships, to ensure that we are at one with those who share our homes and churches and neighborhoods, to transform the "stranger" in those places into persons with names and histories and needs and dreams. It is time to strike the rock, so that healing water may cleanse and cure.

THE DEMANDS OF INTREGRITY

As a child and as a young adult, perhaps no religious practice had the same searing effects on me as that of confession, the sacrament of penance. In pre-Vatican II days, it was customary for Roman Catholics to disappear into the dark confessional on a regular basis, perhaps monthly for laity, weekly for religious. There was a routine about confession, and very often the experience was as innocuous as changing clothes or taking a bath. Sometimes the experience was accompanied by anxiety or fear, especially when I felt I had engaged in some sin that was particularly heinous. In my childhood those were usually sins of impurity. It often seemed to me that the confessor was instantly curious if sins in that category were mentioned. I was convinced the priest had heard none of my routine admissions, but if I mentioned an impure thought or act, there were bound to be questions.

The truth was that not only did I rarely feel forgiven, I often felt more burdened when I exited the little dark box. Surely I was a hypocrite, for I didn't feel that I had seriously violated life's rules, and I didn't feel that I had stirred up God's wrath. Then why was the priest so harsh and so compassionateless? Perhaps I was without hope of redemption, for I knew in my heart of hearts that I would commit again the very acts that Father had just denounced and made me promise never to perform again.

Confession for me was not an experience of mercy and love. It was an obligation and an ordeal. I rarely felt the priest understood me or wanted to help me. I felt defeated, ashamed, and even rebellious. Confession, in that era at least, was confused with telling and forgiveness was a matter of ritual absolution. Implicitly, I longed for an experience that would honor my effort and good will, and would be dignified through warm and sympathetic exchange. God was far more loving than regular confession would suggest. And my heart was deserving of more understanding and affirmation.

That history, which I shared with countless Catholics, helps me to understand why we are less prone today than some

of our Protestant friends to repent openly and easily, in relationships, in liturgy, in prayer in public arenas. We have become very withdrawn and maybe even defensive about our need
for repentance. I used to be amazed when my Anglican friend
spoke of her need to repent or even called me to a moment of repentance. I was often inspired when I heard so many prayer services in ecumenical circles begin with sincere contrition, and a
genuine personal and communal admission of guilt.

How to restore confession to its proper and effective place,
between persons, whether individual or corporate, who have
mutually offended? Though the Roman Catholic church has attempted to personalize the sacrament of penance, many of us
still feel the gap between the transgressions we have committed in our private or social lives, and the neutral, rarified environment of a "confession room." We feel the need to be
reconciled in person (if it is a breach with another person) and
publicly, if we have been guilty of complicity with others in a
social sense. We seek the integrity of honest reconciliation, and
the human signs of restored dignity and reaffirmed trust.

A story is told in Luke's gospel of forgiveness and compassion, a tale of penitence and conversion. Without a doubt it is
also a story of dignity and integrity. There are many messages
lurking in the unfolding of this encounter between Jesus and a
publicly-known sinner. There is the dynamic between Jesus and
Simon, Simon for whom public appearance and reputation
clearly mattered. The dynamic between Jesus and the woman is
one of availability and sincere sorrow. She knew the significance and the impact of a personal gesture, tears, kissing, and
anointing. And Jesus understood her desire to be healed and forgiven. What was it that Simon was chided for? His failure to
be personal and to honor his guest. "You provided no water, you
gave me no kiss, you did not anoint my head." Love, and in this
case, penitent love, is not a matter of words. Human touch con-
veys the heart's desire. Her previous shame and her present
embarrassment did not prevent her from a public display of her
emotions. Jesus was supposed to shun her advances and to reject
her attention. He should have known she was a sinner and

therefore unacceptable. But Jesus' integrity, his openness to a personal relationship, matched the woman's own. And in that exchange, Jesus was honored and the woman was redeemed. The social conventions of the Simons would not allow such forthright behavior, such vulnerability, and such abandoned love.

Our freedom as human beings is grounded in forgiveness, for each of us repeatedly offends and is offended. Each of us is oppressor and oppressed, wounder and wounded. Without the mystery of forgiveness, we are cemented into our roles. We become the sinner, and we cannot free ourselves. Forgiveness liberates us for transformed relationships. The experience of forgiveness enables us to understand our own wretchedness and to accept our failures. We are released to go in peace, to resume our roles as responsible members of the human community.

The exchange between Jesus and the woman reminds us, however, that reconciliation is not a cheap interaction, that it occurs within the context of pain and of sacrifice. There is no alternative to the confrontation with pain: the truth stings. And in most of our human affairs the truth is two-sided. Both parties must bow low and confess. Repentance and forgiveness do not mean the removal of our natural reactions: humiliation, anger, deep hurt, suspicion, mistrust. Rather, they introduce a new patience, a new understanding, a new degree of tolerance, a bending of our pride, all of which are costly. After the price is paid, there is a mysterious and miraculous quieting of the rebellion. Peace creeps in where hostility dwelt, and the human spirit grows in wisdom and maturity. We discover that we have been deliberately holding peace at bay. We, offended and offender, have refused to allow love to enter or be restored. Only when this stubbornness "dies" can love be reborn and renewed.

Forgiveness is therapeutic. At the vulnerable age of thirteen, I was repeatedly abused by a priest. For me it was a frightening experience of sexual initiation coupled with an awe and respect for the ordained clergy. I buried that series of episodes and carried it with me for almost two decades. Then, during therapy, it surfaced. I realized that part of my own growth and self-acceptance depended on removing the obstacle which was my anger and resentment at the indignities this priest had thrust upon me. There was release in the honest letter I wrote to him, baring my own pent-up pain, not accusing or judging, but informing him of the damage he had inflicted. Though I never received a response, the debris left by that tragedy was cleared, and my own integrity was restored.

Each of us must find ways to unblock the streams of life that have been clogged by past traumas and long-forgotten wounds. For some of us, professional analysis must first probe the depths of our psyche and locate the site. For others, the therapeutic ear and heart of a listening friend suffice. The opportunity to pour out one's shame and one's pain, to hear words of forgiveness and reassurance is "confession" at its finest. And confession remains an important part of our lives. It is best if we can speak directly to the person(s) involved, and mutually understand and accept both our actions and their consequences. At least we must find those who can bear with us as we search our way back into harmony with another member of our human community.

We have glimpses in the parable of the prodigal son of both the relief of forgiveness and the barrier of a refusal to forgive. The embrace of the forgiving father healed the haunted and humiliated heart of his son. But the scorn and jealousy of the older brother created a wall that made their common life tense and unbearable.

The key to life in a world of bruises, disappointments, and tragedies is the ability to focus on the blessings restored and the hope engendered, rather than on the past pain and burdens. "In our sadness," writes Ben Weir, "we have been surrounded with the warmth of Christian love and empathy, mediating to us the suffering love of God."[5] Ben and Carol Weir had every reason to question why their daughter had been killed in a bus-train crash, so soon after Ben's release from sixteen months of captivity in Lebanon. We would understand their feelings of despair and anger. Instead their faith and hope inspired ours. Yes, sometimes we are called on to forgive life and life's events, to suspend our questions and our demand for answers. If we don't, we close off the beauties and the blessings that flow even in that time of grief and bewilderment. Only when we pass through the pain and forgive the series of circumstances can we live again in the sun of silent peace and renewed faith.

In that sense forgiveness is a daily challenge. The challenge to let go of our desire to control life, our need to direct outcomes and pre-plan the movements of ourselves and those around us. To let go some of our expectations of others. To let go of weather forecasts, of the interruptions in our carefully scheduled day, of our resentment at an unexpected illness. To "forgive" the failed battery in our car, the untimeliness of someone's request, the long line at the post office, the cold soup, and the erring television screen. If we cannot live at peace amid the disruptions and inadequacies of our daily surroundings, we will hardly be ready to make peace with the more significant wounds and traumas of our life in community. These daily disturbances and challenges provide our training for larger moments in life and for the more demanding crossings-over in love and forgiveness.

Integrity demands that we meet the next moment with a new perception and an open heart, that we leave behind us the dust and the dauntings of former skirmishes and unpleasant encounters. Integrity requires that we reopen the path that disappointment closed and failure barricaded. The challenge to our integrity is that sin and brushes with human weakness, our own and others', can transform us, that contact with the earthiness of our condition rallies us to rejoice in the tolerance and good will of others, that humiliation makes us pliable and understanding, and that truth faced and affirmed frees us for steeper climbs and more dangerous terrain.

FORGIVENESS: THE KEY TO THE DEFEAT OF EVIL

Let us not underestimate the mystery in forgiveness, nor the miracle. Some would say that the act of forgiveness is the key to the defeat of evil, in our small worlds and in our macrocosm as well. As long as hurt is inflicted, or pain proliferated, hostilities and resentments will grow. There will be a human kind of shuttling, from pain to pain, acts of aggression to acts of revenge. The cycle is unending. You hurt my feelings. I resent your callousness and project my pain into another act of vindictiveness, toward you or someone else. The harm increases and the series of acts goes unhalted. It takes one person to arrest the damaging avalanche by offering forgiveness. "Forgiveness grasps the searing stone of sin and will not pass it on."[6] That word or gesture stops the torrent. It dies at that moment. It is taken into and absorbed by the one who renders the forgiving act.

Children's quarrels illustrate the point. An argument begins. You cheated. You cheated first. Names called. Maybe a physical scuffle. Feelings are tense. A division occurs. Each one considers his or her integrity to be challenged. No one will yield, no one will say, "I did cheat," nor, "It doesn't matter; I'm sorry this occurred, and let's make peace."

World powers illustrate the point. You stole our secrets. You cheated on your weapon's agreement. You falsely accused me. You smuggle weapons to our enemies. Name-calling. Threats. Breakdown of all possible peaceful negotiations. Impasse. Stalemate. Cold war. Who will break the cycle? Who will offer a peaceful hand, who will offer a renewed commitment to communicate and return to the negotiating table?

Too often we have believed that forgiveness and reconciliation were signs of weakness. The ideal is to be tough, stand up for yourself, don't give in. Hold your own, our sons and daughters hear us say. Don't let anyone take advantage of you. Grab what you can. Don't be a wimp. Stand firm against terrorists, against communists, against those who would sell their country short. We need a strong defense. Macho mentality. Treat criminals with justice, that is, with harshness. Give the death penalty. I remember still the man some years ago in a small gathering focused on Christian attitudes to war and peace. He spoke of Vietnam. Suddenly he said: "We should have bombed the hell out of the North Vietnamese." There is no greater shame or disgrace than looking weak, than surrendering to the power of another. Somehow the balance between integrity and power, between justice and domination, has been lost. We confuse justice with vengeance and integrity with equality in strength, especially physical strength. A common reaction to the deaths of scores of marines in Beirut a few years ago was: "They should have been tougher." How quick those in charge were to storm the Egyptian airliner in 1986 and meet violence with violence, resulting in fifty-seven, perhaps needless, deaths. Our response to attack is so often attack. Show force, move warships closer, make threats. We have not explored deeply and widely more humane and more effective action.

Few and far between are those political personages who will cross that line of self-justification and superiority, and enter the camp of the opposition to suggest peace. Anwar Sadat did that. McGovern was ridiculed for any such suggestion regarding Vietnam. Can we hope that the tide of hostility will turn or the cycle of violence be broken until our leaders take that route? Until one country says: "We will stop our escalation of arms. We will not test any more nuclear weapons." Until more countries say: "We proclaim ourselves a nuclear-free zone." Until more countries say: "We do not wish to be in the nuclear club." What if most of our young people refused to take part in active combat? What if most of our taxpayers refused to contribute to the defense fund? What if most of us peacemakers or peace-proclaimers were willing to go to jail, as were most of Gandhi's followers? Only then will today's evil be seen for what it is: greed, ruthless power, refusal to acknowledge sin and oppression and injustice.

We all know how hard it is to utter that forgiving word, even in personal contexts. To say: "I'm sorry." To accept the burden of the violence and pain and absorb it into one's own psyche and soul. To refuse to add another sharp jab or justified blow. To discontinue the rounds of revenge and the battle for the last word. To disarm oneself and extend a hand of true forgiveness. We are all sons and daughters of Adam and Eve, and we look for someone to whom we can pass the blame. What would have happened if Adam had said: "I did eat the forbidden fruit and I am sorry?" Or if Eve had said: "I did talk Adam into sinning, and I'm sorry"? "Almost immediately the man and woman face each other in a hostility which can be healed only by mutual forgiveness; but this is not forthcoming."[7]

Perhaps we have to have the experience of a secure and profound bond of love to see that it is possible, and well worth the price. Perhaps only when we sincerely love can we set aside our pride, our need to win, our desire to control or be right, and offer forgiveness, or admit guilt or complicity. Forgiveness may be the highest expression of love, for it is pain that is both born out of and transformed into love. Will those of us who call ourselves Christians reach the point where we acknowledge our complicity in the sins of our society? Or forgive those who have complicated our lives and questioned our veracity by their differing or opposing beliefs? Will we be able to surrender labels and stereotypes, and recognize that the one quality we all have in common is our humanness, with its yearning for wholeness and its proneness to fragmentation? Will we enter the mystery of love and exchange deeply enough so that no one who comes to us will be rejected?

No matter what their sin against us may be, no matter their inability to repent. It may indeed be a path that leads us to the cross. On the road to Gethsemane grace had to overcome nature's reluctance. Grace led Martin Luther King, Jr. down the path where he met an assassin's bullet. Grace led the Ploughshares participants to eight- and ten-year prison sentences, and Dorothy Kazel to a martyr's death in El Salvador. If we take this path seriously, we will have to stop distinguishing between those who are worthy of our forgiveness and those who aren't. Only when pain is met with love does the reign of God open to the person administering the pain. Eventually, we will have to turn our other cheek, not only to those whom we love and respect, but to those who deny us respect and threaten to rob us of dignity and of life. If, that is, we believe that such creative love is the key to the defeat of evil, and the key to the restoration of good will and peace within the human family. In our faith we are called to see ourselves and those who have wronged us within the wide reconciliation of God's realm. In our faith we know that we are not doomed to destroy one another forever.

This is a positive and redemptive response toward pain. If we can contain the pain and refuse to turn it into hatred or revenge, healing can flow to the offender. Then the pain becomes grace, a sacrament of redemption. Is there any greater grace that can occur to one who wrongs another human being than that he or she be forgiven? The estrangement is transformed into reconciliation, the hostility into understanding, the unacceptable becomes acceptable, and the rejected is received. Forgiving one another's sins may be the ultimate sign of our belief that we are all made in the image of God.

A forgiving attitude cannot develop as long as certain other attitudes persist, as long as we cling to our self-righteousness and feed on every opportunity to alienate ourselves and to sit in judgment of others. In Jesus' day the Pharisees epitomized these blocks. "Blind guides! You strain out the gnat and swallow the camel…You erect tombs for the prophets and decorate the monuments of the saints…you are the sons of the prophet's murderers." (Matthew 23:24, 29, 31) "You lay impossible burdens on people but will not lift a finger to lighten them." (Luke 11:46)

How often do we set ourselves up as the determiner of what is acceptable or honorable, place on others higher expectations and greater demands than we put on ourselves? Is our conversation rife with "we" and "they," insuring some alienation? Are we able to pinpoint the speck in another's eye even while we miss the plank that blurs our own vision? Are we too proud to admit mistakes and to say "I'm sorry?" Are our grudges deep and everlasting? Does our own self-esteem depend on squelching and belittling the spirit of another? Have we taken seriously the oft-repeated prayer: forgive us our sins as we forgive others their sins against us?

The consequences of such attitudes stretch from our personal lives far into the international scene, preventing healing and hope, and contributing to the pool of rancor and ill will. The invitation extended to us is the same as that extended to Susanna, falsely accused, or to the father of the prodigal son. That is, to overcome our personal pain and reopen the fountains of life that flow between human beings. To break the chain of sin, degradation, and injury, and forge a new trust. To strike the rock. It is the same invitation that was extended to Mary Magdalen and to Peter. To confess our past, to lay bare our sinfulness and our cowardice, to repent of our failures. To be transformed by the healing power of love, to be made bold in our new integrity. It is the same invitation offered by God to Jesus on Golgotha. To become the place where creative love sculpts a new reality. To bear in our being the unjust wounds and to return to the oppressor the gift of acceptance and mercy. In our day our own grace-filled persons, not the dark confessional, are to be the site of that miraculous exchange.

FIVE

HEALING AND WHOLENESS

"When I first left home, I was so terribly depressed. Drugs of course was my main problem. I did take speed and acid a lot those first weeks. Now I know I can't lean on drugs for the rest of my life. I still smoke pot once in a while, but that's all. Things have started going right for me. I've made some new friends and there is so much beauty in Arizona. I go out in the desert on the motorcycle almost every day after work. I saw an eagle for the first time. I can honestly say now that I'm glad I'm alive."

How easily things get broken! A young life, full of potential and promise, shattered by family disputes, drugs, and their aftermath. This particular young woman dropped out of school and ran away from home. For a time she was hopelessly lost in the syndrome of poverty, drugs, and self-hatred. But in her case there was restoration. In her own time and way she reassembled the pieces of her life and rebuilt the family bonds that had been ruthlessly broken.

Brokenness is a subject each of us understands. The toy we love, the beloved dog that escaped onto the highway that fatal moment. Our injured pride when we don't know the answers. Our grief when we face separations. Losses and setbacks, illness and death, betrayals and loneliness, provide part of the plot of every human story. And so often that fragile peace and sense of well-being are broken suddenly, by impulsive action and careless inattention. Sadness and regret follow. But something is irrevocably different.

The scale and scope of the brokenness of our society are symbolized by police forces, airport security, and defense budgets. Children of broken homes cope with pain and abandonment. Parents grieve over the damage done by drugs. The elderly review sadly their wrecked hopes for a peaceful and secure retirement. Ecology groups lament the careless injuring of the earth. Each of us is able to recite a list of political assassinations in our lifetime.

My own breakdown in 1965 came upon me unexpectedly and with minimal warnings. I was young and responsible and intelligent. My life as a professor and counselor had just begun. I was the newest member of our college philosophy department. My coming had long been awaited by the officials of the college and of my order. I was excited as I reviewed textbooks and exchanged views with other faculty members. My students were eager and responsive. There were long informal discussions with them that made sleep a second choice. And then, how easily things get broken!

I was in a hospital outside the city. The popular diagnosis was "tired nerves." I was bewildered by my own emotional numbness, my failure to regain lost energies. I was slow in recognizing my depression. I slipped further. Something in me was regressing, withdrawing, cutting itself off from all that had constituted vitality and gladness. A third hospital, and even a fourth. I was seriously ill, they told me. I only felt numb. Doctors feared that I was suicidal. I was incarcerated, mistrusted, relegated to the ranks of "mental patient." I had moved in a few short months from a coveted place of honor to the locked ward of a mental hospital. My degree and my inner drive for excellence were not able to save me. I was lost in the cold corridors of my own disoriented and collapsed psyche. Depression broke me. Though I know now it must have been long in coming, the actual shattering seemed quick and total, to myself, and to my disbelieving students, colleagues, friends and family as well. Neither I nor others could find the glue that would repair the damage. We were forced to wait out the slow and painful spread of the depression, and to believe in the equally slow and painful process of healing. It was the most grueling school I had attended. But it changed my life, drastically and forever. No degree or title emerged, but inner harmony and health were my prize.

Too much is broken unnecessarily. We are careless with things we know to be fragile: the earth, human life, peace, relationships, health. But we also know that some brokenness is required, for the secrets of the heart to be revealed. Without some dying—to our addictions, our neurotic possessiveness, our illusionary selves—new life and faith cannot be born. Our failures in love, our ineffective efforts in ministry, our doubts and fears, physical and emotional pain, teach us poverty of spirit, our need for God. When we are struck dumb and blinded by tears, torn apart by conflict, we become suitable places for grace to break through. In our vulnerability and brokenness, we learn the transience and the poignant beauty of life: fallen leaves, a holiday come to an end, the questions in the eyes of a dying friend. We learn the ironies of our aspirins and our martinis, our Fourth of July celebrations, our expensive political campaigns.

Personal and communal scars remind us of the ongoing confrontation with the forces of evil: our amputations, barbed fences, prison walls, slums, and stripped farmlands. We become grateful for the feast of creation, for bread and wine, for the hunger within us for justice, and for every demonstration of reverence for life. We come to each new day mindful of Teilhard de Chardin's morning offering: "This bread, our toil, is of itself but an immense fragmentation; this wine, our pain, is more than a draught that dissolves. Yet, in the very depths of this formless mass you have implanted a desire, irresistible, hallowing, which makes us cry out, believer and unbeliever alike: Lord, make us one."[1] Lord, heal us and make us whole.

This chapter probes the paradox of pain and poignant growth through pain, focusing on the following: 1) suffering and pain as calls to enter more deeply into the world of exchange; 2) healing and our openness to the mystery and flow of exchanged life; 3) rituals of healing; and 4) healing extended to our relationships in society.

A COMMON CUP OF SUFFERING

Rosemary Haughton says: "There is no pain so great as the pain of the soul's longing for God."[2] Most of us do not recognize that pain in our individual experiences of terror and anguish. Most of us do not know ourselves as cosmically situated, as members of one another, transmitting pain to one another as well as relief attempts. Most of us experience our pain as personal, monotonous, and meaningless. We can't voice it adequately, much less place it in the common crucible. And voiceless suffering carried to the extreme becomes suicide, whether instantaneous or drawn out. Our histories, private and communal, resound with muffled pain. Disappointments, losses, diminishments, crowd our days and nights. Holocausts, genocides, famines, catastrophes, strike our borders. We cannot bear the throbbing of our own wounds, and we fear to enter the morass of pain that surrounds us. We respond warily to the one who claims that "God is the memory that forgets no one."[3] So many seem forgotten, so many don't even get into the statistics. We fight the temptation to self-pity and despair. We resist the suggestion that our pain (and rage) is one with all human pain. And that to face it is to cross over into a new phase of our spiritual journey.

Then one experience of pain, survived, and ploughed under, opens up for us the source of a new power, the power to affirm the whole of reality, the cross and the resurrection. To affirm the enduring qualities of love and compassion. To affirm the transcendence of life and its invincibility. We enter the dark regions of our own life, and our helplessness before others' pain, with more sensitivity, with more discipline, and with a new strength. Our silence and our grief lead to repentance. And repentance reunites us with all who suffer. United, we gain courage, to face our complicities with the demons who pursue and possess us. We acknowledge that at the center of us there will be an ongoing pain, a cosmic ache, for healing and redemption, for God's realm to break through and transform our human existence. We know that the cup will not be removed. The test of our identification with Jesus is that we drink the same bitter cup that he drank, that we carry our share of suffering as ransom for one another. All life in God's realm, says Charles Williams, is to be vicarious.[4] All suffering, individual and cosmic, is part of the system of exchange. When we suffer alone, we are doomed to a lonely hell. When we share our suffering, we exchange healing and strength as well.

From my twenty years perspective, I look back in awe at the process of healing that gave me back my life. Time was an important factor. Time seemed to have stopped altogether, and I languished in a dark room of vague entrances and exits, with no thoughts and no feelings and no plans. Each day began as a burden, moved endlessly through a series of necessary routines, and ended in continued meaninglessness. I am not so quick now to underestimate the therapy of time. For at some point I began to notice the sunshine as I woke in the morning. I felt the wind brushing through my hair as I walked. I felt a spark of interest in world events and in conversations around me. Colors were alive again, and days different from one another. Once again I could concentrate as I read a book or composed a letter. "Thus says the Lord God to these bones: See! I will bring spirit into you, that you may come to life." (Ezekiel 37:5)

Two personal qualities assisted my restoration: stubbornness and faith. I refused to let go of the thin thread that connected me to life pulsing around me. I refused to accept the judgment that an emotional breakdown would destroy me forever. I fought for recognition that I and my co-sufferers were human beings and only a shade different from many of my respected visitors. In fact, sometimes we were more honest and more in touch with unspoken realities. I fought to be released from that hospital ward which was even more depressing than my own inner misery. I fought to begin some meaningful work, before I was ready; after a relapse, I fought again. When my doctor was discouraged that my condition had reached a plateau, and I was

failing to reach the milestones of recovery, I still had faith.
Even in the most desolate periods, I knew that there was some
reason for this darkness. When others suggested I make some
new life-choices—leave the Franciscans, for example, undergo
shock treatment as a last resort—when I could barely endure
the necessary rituals of face-washing and dressing and regular
eating, I still believed. I not only believed, I knew I wanted to
write, to tell this tale, even while it was incomplete, to redeem
this time and this experience. My doctor was both amused and
convinced. And on the power of that move toward self-
determination, I entered a new stage of my recovery.

The third factor in my healing was the solid and steadfast
support of those who waited with me. There weren't many: perhaps I wouldn't allow many. Some were too fearful to even pre-
tend that they could wait with me. I was too much of an
embarrassment to them and too much of a burden. But those who
stood on the fringes, as near as I allowed them, were faithful.
And because they passed every test that I could administer,
they convinced me that they cared. And if they cared, I must be
someone worth caring for. On the strength of that logic, I tot-
tered my way back into the ranks of the healthy.

My doctor in particular succeeded in opening a door inside
me. Through it came the flow of energy I needed, and from my
deepest inner recesses there stirred a responding energy. If it is
true that others can give us birth by breathing over us until we
are sure enough of our capacity to breathe, he mothered my new
life.

That period covered the better part of three years. It is now
integrated into my life and has been succeeded by many diverse
and rich experiences, deep and lasting relationships, a variety
of ministries, and countless opportunities for learning, travel,
and adventure. But I never feel far from the revelations of that
time. In fact, as I write these lines, I feel a bit of cold sweat and
a restriction in my chest. I am still frightened and in awe of the
tremendous capacities of the human psyche for both despair
and ecstasy.

It may never be easy for me to remember that bleak cell of

depression with its hollow walls and disturbing vacuums. Some time ago I saw a duck flying across a lagoon near my home, with an arrow through its wing. It flew nonetheless. I have watched the fields around me as they are harvested and as the earth is plowed under, preparation for the winter and next year's sowing. Trees are phenomenal in their ability to begin again from the tiniest shoot of green on a dead trunk. Life is wistful and rimmed with dangers. We are frail creatures and easily broken. But we are all sturdy and dependable in our struggle for life. Healing is mysterious and elusive. But it always remains a possibility while hearts still beat and hope persists. I have deep faith in our inner human desire for healing and renewal. And this applies to the most broken among us: the chronic alcoholic, the disturbed adolescent, the depressed, the rebellious, the despairing.

The Psalms express in vivid images and with anguishing truth the cries of those who await healing. They are the litanies of the chronically ill, the oppressed, the forgotten, the fearful. For people of faith there is the assurance that God has not abandoned them, even in dire experiences of torture and desertion. That belief sustains them.

Who are the main characters of the gospels? The blind, the lame, the lepers, the possessed, and the paralyzed. Mothers of dead children, Mary the prostitute, Peter the betrayer. Jesus offered healing, it seems, only when there was a sign from the one suffering that he or she believed. Jesus emphasized this dynamic repeatedly. "Your faith has healed you." "Why are you lacking in faith?" "He could work no miracle here…so much did their lack of faith distress him."

In our own day of agnosticism and sophisticated religion, many bypass the Psalms and regard cynically the numerous accounts of miraculous cures in the gospels. The pleas of the former are too simple and the narratives of the latter too spectacular. Many miss the underlying message of the necessity of a naked faith, a faith humble enough to plead, a faith honest enough to acknowledge one's deepest and most personal needs. The faith expressed by many of our national leaders is often a proud faith, a covering for a bold belief in our own powers and our own ability to control any situation. We have faith in our efficiency, our technology, our rate of progress. We have faith in our weapons, our intelligence systems, our investments. But when the spaceship Challenger explodes before our eyes, we are silent. When terrorists strike a blow at our vulnerability, force is our first solution. When a nuclear accident occurs, we continue to deny the dangers. We will not be brought to our knees and to the realization that we are sinful and self-righteous. We seek not healing, but face-saving and revenge.

Individuals also put their faith in real estate, in their promotions, in science, and in themselves. When tragedy flattens their family, they are bankrupt. When illness threatens their life, they frantically seek the best medical treatment, regardless of cost or availability. When they are thwarted in their business or their ambitions, they resort to illegal practices or outright injustice. Corporate life is described as a rat race, the competition is cut throat. Marriage is old-fashioned, and fidelity is for the scrupulous.

This value system has even seeped into our churches. One United States denomination freely admitted that they wanted their church headquarters to be located in a city with a certain image. A Roman Catholic bishop spends extravagant amounts of money on his installment ceremony and on his episcopal residence. Many clergy fear to speak the truth to their congregations lest they lose the contributions of their wealthiest members. It is not healing we seek for our waywardness, but greater security for our current way of life. What might Jesus have meant: "But when the Human One comes, will he find any faith on the earth?" (Luke 18:8)

THE MYSTERY OF HEALING

We are witnessing in our day, in some countries especially, the growth of charismatic communities and the popularity of healing sessions. I was involved in a discussion on the condition of the church in Great Britain, and asked where one might see signs of renewal. I was directed to the charismatics. In another similar discussion, someone claimed that the healing ministry was the greatest sign of hope for today's church. Both comments interest me. While I can acknowledge that some mysterious healings are authentic and undeniable, I have always been uncomfortable with charismatics, and skeptical of the crowds that gather around a faith healer. When I spoke face to face with a Methodist faith healer from Sri Lanka, I found myself tolerating his stories and suspending my belief. Yet in my heart I was suspicious of the power of his personality over the simple-hearted people who came to him for help.

Each time I am exposed to stories of healing by the laying on of hands, or by the reading of hearts, I shudder a bit and retreat into my incredulity. Perhaps some of my reaction is due to the dominant role played by male clergy ministering to women. But I also understand something of this phenomenon, and have my own explanation for the growth of interest in miracle healings. If it is true that agnosticism is a strong characteristic of our society, and that matters of faith and of mystery are viewed with cynicism if not outright scorn, then it is natural that an opposite trend will also develop, a trend toward belief in miraculous occurrences. So many people have been deprived of an informed faith, of opportunities to probe and examine their religious practices and beliefs, that they are in fact starved for experiences of the world of the spirit. Some of today's developments are giving them access to that faith, and giving them as well a sense of belonging to a caring community. I do not want to dismiss the potential and actual miracles that do occur in these circles. But I search these caring communities for more conscious links to other efforts, to groups who seek socially and politically for responses to human pain.

Having said that with distanced caution, I add that I was partially converted by a personal experience. I went to church one Sunday entirely oblivious of a planned healing service. My heart was heavy with pain from a misunderstanding with someone I loved. When we were invited forward to indicate the nature of our need for healing, I did so. Two members of the congregation prayed over me and over my absent friend, and anointed me for the journey of reconciliation. In all honesty, I felt its effects, and when I shared the experience with that friend, the breakthrough occurred. Our tears confirmed our mutual forgiveness.

Recently I was privileged to join a group of incoming patients for their orientation at the Bristol Cancer Clinic in England. Each person seeking treatment brought a friend or relative. As we shared our fears about cancer and our hopes for healing, it was abundantly clear that healing included far more than the physical reduction of a tumor or the remission of that dreaded disease. While the patients voiced their needs, the staff confirmed the Clinic's commitment to offer opportunities for spiritual and emotional healing, even in those cases where physical healing might not be possible. I learned something about the possibility of being healed on one's way through death, of a deeper healing that transforms the experience of death. Once again I was called to openness to the multidimensions of the healing mystery.

In the United States recently, the film *Agnes of God* drew unusually large crowds. People seemed to be fascinated by this controversial film, at the same time wanting to reject it as bizarre and unbelievable. The film's story revolves around the innocence or guilt of a young novice, who seemingly has murdered her newborn baby. Underlying that investigation is the further question of the baby's conception, which remains in mystery. The implication exists that possibly, the baby did not have a human father. The effort of the baffled and caring psychiatrist, who is a woman, is to save this young woman from the protected and crippling environment of the convent. For me, regardless of the artistic strengths or weaknesses of the film, there is a comment on our times. In our world of science and research and rationality, is there any room for mystery and for faith? Who and what might bridge the gap we all feel at times between our mechanical, straightforward lives and those inexplicable moments of contact with powers and presences that cannot be verified? Faith is a mystery, and I confess that too often I, too, try to reduce it to logic and problem-solving.

RITUALS OF HEALING

Many activists in the United States were disturbed to hear that Helen Caldicott had announced her retirement from her role in the peace movement. She had been an invaluable leader as head of the organization, Physicians for Social Responsibility. In an interview she gave several reasons for her withdrawal, among which was her own need for healing. She had been burned out by an exacting schedule and its heavy demands. She wanted to take time to paint bits of the planet that she loves and has long worked to save, to read the messages of Gandhi and of Jesus, to garden, to be with her own and other children. By her own words, these activities were sacraments of healing for her.

On hearing this, I was reminded of the rituals of healing that are personally restoring, and that we have incorporated into our social and religious lives. A handshake or an embrace after a difficult exchange represents a kind of healing. An open hand or arms signify our desire for reconciliation. Sometimes talking is healing, when we have a compassionate listener, or returning to the scene of our pain and allowing it to speak all its messages once again. Sometimes an embrace is the only language we have to address another's pain and suffering. Our eyes are powerful instruments of healing, as well. With a glance Jesus accused Peter of his betrayal. With a glance Jesus reached out on the cross to heal the brokenness of John and of his mother. Similarly, how many people have waited in anguish and hope at a bedside for a last look of acceptance, forgiveness?

Down the centuries we have practiced anointing, the strengthening gesture of confirmation, the forgiving gesture of the remittance of sin, holy oils to heal the ailing body. Always there is a recognition of the importance of touch, of human contact to reassure and reunite.

In our need, as in the case of Helen Caldicott, we seek those activities and those situations that heal our weary bodies and spirits. One may find healing in a novel, digging in the garden, or listening to classical music; another in a solitary walk through the park. Some turn to the scriptures or to meditation, or even to a humorous film. Space itself is my antidote for weariness and discouragement, finding a place outdoors where the wind can get at me, where I can see a distant horizon, and where I can begin to know, within and without, the slow return of freedom. We need to discover those healing places and moments, then claim them for our own. Each is an experience of exchange with the world about us and its restorative forces. They are the sacraments of life, the keys to unlocking fresh supplies of energy and peace.

Our very wounds and scars—when they have been healed enough and carefully woven into the fabric of our lives, when they have been transformed into marks of love and compassion—can be instruments of healing for one another. Our mourning for a loved one can lead us to reintegrate that person's life back into our own and into life around us, to ensure the continuation of his or her vitality and meaning. The ease and freedom with which we accept our physical disabilities enables others to face their own deficiencies. Jesus invited Thomas to touch his wounds so that his doubt might be healed. Christians everywhere take heart from the witness of scars and the suffering they represent. Martyrs are honored from year to year. The agonizing testimonies from Latin America heal us of some of our divisiveness and pettiness. Contact with political prisoners and refugees strengthens us for mission. Perhaps our scars are the most important gifts we have to offer each other, signs of our common condition, signs of the creative power of suffering.

A priest I once knew was an eloquent example. He was severely diabetic and virtually blind, dependent on others for things we all take for granted. He was not able to drive, he couldn't read, and he often couldn't identify who was addressing him. Nevertheless, he worked as a chaplain in a mental hospital. He understood the pain of those people; he was patient and sensitive. He made his own wounds available, with a remarkable kind of humor, to all he met. He didn't take himself too seriously and he took time for unusual things: picking flowers, visiting friends, playing with children. He liked gaudy vestments. He was human and warm and piercingly truthful.

His own disabilities stripped him, it seemed, of the need for facades. He saw life, especially the fragile lives of those around him, as an amazing gift. He never excluded himself from the ranks of the wretched, the lost, and the blind, who had, by grace, been saved.

So often, healing has to do with forgiveness. Forgiveness of oneself, for failures and limitations. For not being as virtuous or as successful as a peer or a colleague. For having made a disaster of a marriage or of someone's life. For not having acted when one should have or for having acted when one should not have. For surviving when others have died.

And mutual forgiveness. The circle formed by human relationships, individuals and groups, is a symbol of wholeness, of completion. When the circle is broken, we feel division and damage inside, as well as in our shared life. Most often that circle is healed by forgiveness. A new level of acceptance and understanding. A new discovery of the depths of love. A renewed desire to be mutually formed and transformed. The greater tragedy occurs when the circle is broken and we don't feel the pain of the severance, or we become accustomed to it. Many of us as Christians do not feel pain or diminishment in the face of our separation. We do not feel the need for forgiveness from one another. And we do not yearn enough for our mutual transformation.

If we find ourselves or another unforgivable, the wound will remain. Healing, then, will only be superficial. Exchange will be limited, and eventually the channels of giving and receiving will harden and close. Sometimes the power to forgive another is hard to come by. We have to strain and suffer and beg for guidance. Sometimes we must wait for years for the miracle to occur within us. Like the Masai tribe in Tanzania, we have to pray that the "spittle of forgiveness" will come. Spittle was considered the sign of acceptance and reconciliation. When it came, there was great rejoicing in the whole community,[5] for the whole community is affected by any broken bonds within it.

We have all witnessed or experienced that moment when

hearts open again to one another, eyes meet, and healing rushes in to bind up old wounds. I remember a poignant moment when a young friend and I sat, aching and strained, by a stream. We both hoped that we might reopen the closed door and find entrance once more in each other's trust. But it didn't come. We spoke polite words, we looked past each other, and we walked our separate ways, deprived of each other's blessing. The wound is still alive, six years later. And I still pray that the spittle will come.

THE WIDER WOUNDS OF SOCIETY

Among the areas of human life today where we are challenged to find new images and patterns of healing, a few call out for specific mention. The dominant world-view of our western society is one of alienation and division. Beings, human beings in particular, are seen as superior and inferior, as valuable and less valuable. The valuable are those with power, wealth, and prestigious positions. The less valuable are the poor, the homeless, and the uneducated. We have managed to be extremely objective and impersonal about these distinctions. The first group for the most part espouses equal opportunity, universal freedom, human rights, and human dignity. But they enclose themselves in separate lifestyles, separate schools, neighborhoods, clubs, even churches. Their distance from the lower part of the pyramid is symbolized by jet planes, private swimming pools, and multiple credit cards.

One mark of that separation is male dominance. In the United States poverty has become increasingly feminine. In India an alarming percentage of suicide victims are women. In many parts of Africa women's only claim to distinction is their ability to bear children. In Latin America there are slow changes in the macho mentality and the continued domestication of women. Related to this is society's dominant consciousness of a God who is male, and the complicity of some churches in denying the gifts and experience of women. The gospel message continues to be distorted by culturally-bound structures and mindsets.

Though they have been criticized for not going far enough and for not always practicing their own teaching, the United States Catholic bishops have begun to heal some of the deep splits in traditional ways of thinking. Other church leaders have done the same. Economic justice and world peace are now subjects of morality and social responsibility. But all too frequently the splits remain obvious: politics and spirituality, Sundays and weekdays, religion and life. An Anglican vicar was baffled when I asked his congregation's reaction to the constant barrage of United States bombers overhead, and to what degree they were involved in the Campaign for Nuclear Disarmament. A young woman I met recently, who works as a missionary with a fundamentalist group in Brazil, had not even heard of *communidades de base.* My community is constantly criticized for concerning itself with issues that are not "appropriate" for religious women. Numerous women occupying the pews in our churches have no difficulties with an all-male clergy, with sexist language in song and scripture, with the dearth of female voices and female insights in church affairs and matters of faith. Fortunately, that is slowly changing.

A spirituality based on exchange proclaims the coming of a new community where no gifts are ignored, a community in which there is ongoing reflection on its contradictions and ambiguities, constant experiment with new styles of sharing authority and discerning ministry. This spirituality proclaims a consciousness of God as relational, and life as whole and interdependent. In our own situations and cultures, we women must reclaim our history and correct the discrepancies in our lives. We must enter our true identity "as carriers of relatedness, of feeling values, and of the quiet nourishing qualities of the earth."[6] Together with men who believe in a just and caring society, we must heal our own false socialization, reject hierarchical images wherever they occur, and take responsibility for modeling relationships and communities that are personal, mutually respectful, and authentically human.

Our hierarchical conditioning has been particularly effective in separating clergy and laity. What will bridge the long-term chasm that has been created, between the ordained with a monopoly on authority, on power, and on expertise in matters of faith; and the non-ordained, convinced of their dependence and second-rate status? Presumably the Second Vatican Council righted some of that in my church. And yet I find places in my own country, and in India, in Germany, in Great Britain, where the old patterns are as sacred and untouchable as ever.

A spirituality of exchange calls us all to holiness, and calls us all to ministry. If we are a priestly people, we are all required to perform pastoral duties: we are all empowered to interpret our faith. The spiritual life is a pilgrimage and we need one another, for mutual nourishment and for mutual correction. We need rituals and devotions that are more related to the sacraments of life and to scripture, and less dependent on obligation and on ecclesiastical approval. The center of this spirituality is the cell in the world, the family, the community, the emerging new church, and not in the chancery, not in the monastery. We as laity must acknowledge that we have been deprived of our rightful heritage. We must refuse to be given the short shrift and pacified. We must have confidence in our own ministries, which include leading worship, serving as spiritual directors, and bringing life and meaning to the gospels. Rather than abandon our churches, we must reclaim them and make collegiality with our ordained brothers a reality. It is time to honor the lay saints: Gandhi, Dorothy Day, E.F. Schumacher, Jean Donovan, Elie Wiesel, Rosa Parks.

And finally, an insidious effect of our conditioning is to separate us from our authentic selves. We are encouraged to fit into this divided society by dividing ourselves: valuing our intellectual achievements and dismissing our practical abilities, having one code of behavior in our jobs and another in our church participation, separating spirituality and sexuality, truth and polite intercourse. We are too busy developing our careers to enjoy our middle years or to discover our unique gift of poetry or photography. We shrink from calling our physical cycles and our emotional outbursts holy. We neglect sides of our personality: the clown, the child, the contemplative, while we invest all our energies into our organizations and our five-year plans. We doubt that love means prayer together as well as physical intimacy. We miss the living connection between "women for peace" and our yearning for deeper prayer, between our anti-apartheid rallies and our unintegrated congregations. We speak of being world citizens while we view life from the perspective of our own cultures. We confuse wholeness with self-sufficiency, and exchange with control.

The spirituality we seek wends a new path through our conventions and our traditional dichotomies. It encourages us to love the distance between us, as well as the dance that connects us. It endorses holidays as well as retreats. It urges us to use our imaginations as well as to practice discipline. To move gracefully between our own solid and peaceful center, and the circles that both feed and drain us. To live in the unique and vivid here and now rather than in the obligations of the past or the abstractions of the future. To choose the truth in our hearts over the social conventions and the psychological games that are thrust at us. To become channels of healing as our lives become more whole and wholesome.

The gospel pages are narrations of brokenness and healing: Zacchaeus, the son of the official, the daughter of Jairus, the lepers, the woman at the well. They are parallels for our own stories of brokenness and contain clues to the way to healing. Don't be afraid to face the truth. Don't return to patterns of behavior proved false. Don't miss the moment of healing. Don't underestimate the power of human touch and human caring. Don't forget to be thankful. Don't consider your healing the end of your search. Present yourself as you are, with all your sordidness and selfishness, your checkered past and your weak resolve. Put guilt to rest and enter into the challenges of the present moment. Be more conscious of your unique responsibilties and your undisputed worth. Go more than halfway in your willingness to repent and boldly announce your need and your sorrow. Be patient with yourself and with those who have hurt you. Be compassionate even when you feel like withdrawing. Put your own hurts at the service of those in greater suffering. Rejoice in each breakthrough and celebrate each occasion of new life. Take healing as your mission.

Regardless of our life's work, we are each called to the ministry of reconciliation and wholeness. We are strangers and aliens no longer. We form a household, a body. We are members of one another, one in our helplessness, our pain, and our desire for wholeness. We are potential instruments of peace. It is conceivable that we could yet become a community in which no person suffers totally alone. "I know of no other activity which is as revolutionary and as healing as the creation of friendships within which we talk with each other about what really matters to us. . . .After all, what is there to do in the wilderness, except pull up a rock and talk with each other?"[7]

It will take courage to see beyond our own sufferings. "The souls on Dante's mountain, while they never allow themselves to be distracted from the pain and tension which awareness of the shadow brings, yet give to the travellers as they pass their full attention, with such of their faculties as are free to hear, to see, or to speak."[8] May we have the grace to live with those wounds that can't be healed. And wounded as we are, may we take up our sacred task, to become the rivers that run the length and width of our world where healing flows.

SIX

PRAYER AND PRESENCE

"People sometimes refer to me as living alone and in some sense that is true. But in the last years your presence has become a permanent reality. That is a kind of secret I can't easily explain to folks. Your support and friendship are grace for me no matter where you are. They help to close the gaps of time and distance."

Closing the gaps of time and distance! That is as accurate a description as any of the activity we call praying. We step outside of time, for a moment or longer, and we move into eternity, where history is now, where what we fear can be unmasked, where what we hope for can be experienced. We lose a sense of our limitations and our spirits encompass the world, traveling easily to the people and needs that occupy our hearts and minds.

God is not contained in time or place. How mysterious God's omnipresence was to us as children! God followed us into the darkness and waited for us exactly where we thought we were alone. We couldn't hide from God; our secret actions were scrutinized and judged. At six and at twelve, we narrowed that God-quality to something negative and frightening. Perhaps now in a more mature time, we welcome the experience of an omnipresent Spirit, as we pray that God's realm will come and that our daily bread will be shared with children in São Paulo and Khartoum. As we bring together in intention, if not in human encounter, Palestinians and Israelis, terrorists and their hostages, right-wing death squads, and young freedom fighters.

It seems to me that prayer and presence are inseparable, that to pray means to enter into the presence of. To be present is enough for prayer. Is that what St. Paul meant when he said: "Pray unceasingly"? Be mindful to whom you belong and keep before your gaze those who are forgotten, those who suffer and cry out, those joined to you by ties of blood and faith and love.

I had my most memorable lesson in the prayer of presence during my first sojourn in India. Geographically speaking, I was acutely aware of distance and differences. The West, my familiar world of highways and architecture, of customs and comforts, seemed remote. Letters traveled slowly and were jumbled in their order of arriving. Day was night in my native land. Malayalam words and music threatened to drown out my own hymns and prayer responses. In the midst of that foreign environment, the Psalms and the images of scripture came alive. I saw the women at the well. I cast my eyes to the mountains. I observed the shepherd with his flock. In my hands I held the mustard seed and the grain of wheat. I walked the dusty roads and washed my feet with a sense of ritual. People around me picked up their mats after a night under the open skies.

The parables, the beatitudes, and the accounts of the Passion took on new meaning and Indian flesh as I prayed on the convent rooftop, in the ruins of a Buddhist monastery, and under the shade of a centuries-old rock. God was present to me in myriads of stars, in daily rice, in curious eyes. God wore the clothes of Indian peasants, was barefoot, and often hungry. God moved slowly by ox cart, was revealed in the quiet sunset, and through the healing hands of sister nurses. God spoke a new language and asked unusual questions. And among all this newness and surprise, God was present in the love and support of those I had left behind. I experienced their presence in an unusually vivid manner. I knew their concern and their encouragement. I was physically and psychically buoyed by the realization that I was sent, accompanied and comforted by those who loved me. It was a miracle of exchange, I in India, they in distant lands. Our lives intertwined, my experience flowing out to them, their strength fortifying me. Both my surroundings in India and my support group at home were sacraments of presence and of communion. Time and distance faded away. Prayer and presence closed the gap.

Presence is now and forever. "I am with you always," Jesus told his disciples at the very moment he was to leave them. They are haunting words, words that perhaps require a lifetime before we penetrate their meaning and experience the fullness of their power. Indeed, we go from level to level in our understanding of presence. Often, unique moments in our lives lead us through these transitions. A night of lonely agony and the very real awareness of a supporting hand. A long separation and the reassuring echoes of a laugh, a shared scripture passage, a private language. A misunderstanding, with its haunting hurt and desire for forgiveness. A shared mission on distinct soils and the belief in a common journey and a joint pilgrimage. It was Jesus' farewell gift to his friends. It is the miracle of here and now amid the reality of separation and distance. Gibran says, "When you part from your friend, you grieve not; for that which you love most in him [sic], may be clearer in his absence, as the mountain to the climber is clearer from the plain."[1]

In Revelation 3:20 we read: "Here I stand, knocking at the door. If anyone hears me calling and opens the door, I will enter...have supper." Implicit in the invitation is the notion of prayer as presence, as sacrament, and as the opportunity for exchange. Once we acknowledge 1) that prayer is not an escape or a panacea, we can explore, 2) the power of presence, 3) the dailiness of prayer as sacrament, and 4) the fruitfulness of its exchange.

QUESTIONS ABOUT PRAYER

Do the people around you understand this experience of presence and its relationship to prayer? Are we sufficiently able to offer this gift of presence to our world and our times? How do we restore the meaning of Jesus' words, "I am with you always," to those who are alone and afraid, to those who mistrust and despair, to the faithless and the cynics?

One summer I helped to prepare for a conference on ecumenical spirituality. Those living the vowed life in community were the focus of this particular consultation. How did an Orthodox monk, a Reformed nun, a Catholic Benedictine, view the relevance of their lives for others seeking meaning and purpose in life? What kind of prayerful exchange could justify the amount of resources and people's energies invested in the monastic life? What is the relationship between prayer and the human suffering that surrounds us? They were difficult questions for the participants. The quality of our prayer life leads us immediately into the matter of exchange. Is not our prayer a journey to the borders, the place where we become the bridge between two worlds? That endeavor requires a high degree of sensitivity and vulnerability.

Much is revealed about the quality of our prayer as we take a survey of our churches and communities. How many of the descriptions that follow resonate with your own experience? On the one hand we meet "easy," almost glib, prayer, sometimes spontaneous, often read from prepared texts. We make grand offerings and are nearly oblivious to the gap between our words and our intended action. On the other side, we meet apathy and cynicism. Prayer, some say, is a naive exercise, and presence is a mere poetic expression. Weary of unimaginative repetition and of sterile ritualism, the agnostics in our midst resort to sarcasm.

Sometimes we fall into the trap of organizing prayer as we would organize a speech or a conference agenda. In our multiple papers and our efforts to follow a theme, we lose the elements of spontaneity and of mystery that are the entrance points for the Spirit. One of the worst incidents of organized prayer I've experienced occurred in Assisi. I was with friends in a chapel in Santa Chiara waiting for a liturgy to begin. We were grateful for a bit of silence and for a little respite from Assisi's crowds. We were startled when an eerie feminine voice suddenly began reciting a litany, with appropriate pauses for an anonymous response. Only a voice, no face. And then we realized it was a tape-recorded message, a prayer that could be played at any time and that required no human attendance and no sense of presence. For me, it was the epitome of non-prayer. Something similar happens in one of the downtown churches where I sometimes go for weekday Eucharist. As soon as the liturgy has ended, before anyone has an opportunity to pause and savor the action just engaged in, a voice from somewhere near the back of church begins the recitation of the rosary. If you wish to pray alone or in silence, you must leave the church.

Speaking is often the medium of our prayer, rather than listening. Where in our prayer experiences do we allow time for the Spirit to stir the waters, for the Word to seep into our minds and hearts? And where, in the style of the Quakers, do we invite and encourage one another to minister to each other, by sharing the fruits of our meditation and our inner enlightening? We are prone to plan and to program our prayer, placing limits on the action of the Spirit. We are less concerned about preparing docile and quiet hearts.

Sometimes our prayer circles become places of discussion. Afraid to bare ourselves to one another or to God, to be simple in our needs and offerings, we cloak our prayer in lofty quotations poorly cited, in logical displays of our spiritual erudition, and in platitudes that we never intend to enflesh. Sterile and even arrogant, such prayer attempts. We talk about the Scriptures, analyze and speculate on them, rather than confess that the challenge they offer is beyond our strength. Our prayer lacks flesh and blood, honesty and truth.

Experiences with children remind us vividly of this ingredient. One of my friends taught inner-city seven year olds, and they began their day with spontaneous prayer. The petitions might go as follows: "For my uncle, so that he doesn't beat up my aunt." "So that we can stay in the United States and not get deported." Not only children can remind us. One of my sisters says quite simply: "You are going to be traveling a lot in the next months. I will place you each day under Psalm 121." She knows which psalm fits the needs of those she loves. She follows us into situations foreign to her, but made familiar by her breathing of the psalms. And there is the ninety year old in a nursing home who tells me she prays for me by name every day. It is her missionary activity and her gift to me. I often remember that as I sit in a planning meeting, or board a plane, or undertake a new assignment, and I draw on the promised strength and reassurance.

Those who ask about our prayer deserve an answer. Our times call us to look seriously at the quality and the meaning of our prayer. Prayer is not a luxury, an escapist exercise, a panacea for our personal miseries. It is a step into a world of intangible relationships, of gratuitous exchange. It is a commitment to strike the rock, to go to the borders and be a go-between.

PRAYER AS PRESENCE

Prayer—its meaning, style, and content—is determined by our conception of who God is. We look to Jesus' relationship with God and we see how that bond affected the whole of Jesus' prayer, in word and in action. Authentic worship is not bound by place or custom. It is authentic because it is of the Spirit and within the framework of truth. Such was Jesus' proclamation to the Samaritan woman. Her narrow notions of addressing God and paying respect to God were broken open by Jesus' announcement that God is Spirit and holy by nature, not by virtue of anything we contribute in our devotion or by our clever requests. Similarly, Jesus dismissed the money changers because they polluted what was to be a holy presence. How to strip our prayer and our attitudes of all false accretions and to stand simply in God's presence! How to recognize that presence in "the holy" that surrounds us: the quiet of a sunbathed meadow, the grandeur of a centuries-old cathedral, the simplicity of an oriental prayer circle, the confusion of a crowded Latin barrio.

Who needs our elaborate preparations and our liturgically correct rubrics, God or us? Who is honored by the same? Rituals and ceremonies are to facilitate and deepen our sense of spirit and truth as we enter worship, not to distract and detour us.

Jesus' relationship with God (whom he called "Father," in the intimacy that word evoked in his Jewish tradition) was direct and transparent. "The Father and I are one." "I do what he commands me." "If it is possible, let this cup pass from me." "Your word is truth." It is as if Jesus tells us over and over again: If only you could know how much God loves, how much God longs to be central in your life, how eager God is to welcome and forgive and refresh you. "I will ask and God will give you another Paraclete" to be with you always, the Spirit of truth, the Holy Spirit, the giver of life and hope and energy. All the gifts of God: the glory of creation, the marvels of human existence, the mysteries of love and friendship and fidelity, the promise of peace and justice in a new society, are summarized in this gift of the Spirit.

On another occasion, in speaking of prayer, Jesus reminds us that surely human parents do everything in their power to give good gifts to their children. How much more then will God give this Holy Spirit to all of us, beloved children! How do we become like little children in our attitudes to God in prayer? How do we let go of our adult hangups and our adult sense of independence and self-sufficiency and ask for, plead for, the things we need and the gifts that others need? Can we come to the simple belief that intercession is the beloved child's way of speaking to a parent? Can we believe that in moments when we lift up our needs, and especially the needs of our brothers and sisters, we are opening ourselves to the life and energy and power of the Holy Spirit? In those moments we are connecting and bonding in a unique way. And can we believe that the effects of that bond extend to and are felt by those whom we name, whether they know us and rely upon us, or whether they would even consent to such inclusion? Charles Williams describes such intercession in *The Greater Trumps:* "She emptied her mind of all thoughts and pictures. She held it empty till the sudden change in it gave her the consciousness of the spreading out of the stronger will within; then she allowed that now unimportant daily mind to bear the image and memory of Nancy into its presence. She did not in the ordinary sense 'pray for' Nancy; she did not presume to suggest to Omniscience that it would be a thoroughly good thing if it did; she merely held her own thought of Nancy stable in the midst of Omniscience. She hoped Nancy wouldn't mind if she knew."[2]

Robert Hugh Benson tells of a person who chanced upon a lonely chapel where a nun was praying. To that passer-by the whole world seemed to be revolving around that secluded, unlikely place with its single, frail advocate. The nun's simple prayer, embracing the world, was seen to be the source of its animation and its sustenance.[3] When we believe in and receive the power of the Spirit without qualification, we become such a center of life, radiation, and energy. "Maybe journey is not so much a journey ahead or a journey into space, but a journey into presence. The farthest place on earth is the journey into the presence of the nearest person to you."[4]

This God of Jesus is a faithful God. "The One who sent me is with me. God has not deserted me." (John 8:29) Neither in time of temptation nor suffering. Neither in the mottled history of the church, nor in our contemporary search. Neither in the El Salvadorans' journey toward liberation nor in the South Africans' resistance to oppression. Neither in Pilate's courtroom nor on the Mount of Golgotha. Neither in Ita Ford's last struggle nor in the dying moments of the latest AIDS victim. I am with you always. Present to you, accompanying you, leading the way. It is that realization of faith that enables all of us to find comfort and strength on our daily journey. Whether we cry out from our hospice bed or whether we take our place in a monotonous factory. Whether we harvest rice in South India or whether we teach native American children in northern Wisconsin. Whether we count our blessings or bless our unyielding fields. Whether we dread the future or prepare for our own death. It is the mystery of relatedness and presence, the gift of the Holy Spirit, uniting us to one another in an unbreakable bond and gathering us to our God in an inclusive embrace.

How we pray, what we say, and what we experience as fruit all depend on our conception of who God is. God as truth, God as giver of life and gift, God as faithful: this is the God of

Jesus. Present to us in the Word of scripture, in the wisdom of our daily discerning, in the nakedness of our own inner spirit. Present to us in wind and sky, in food and fellowship, in miracles of healing, and in times of tenderness and of celebration. Present to us in struggle and defeat, in loneliness and lapses, in ordeals of decision making and of betrayal. From these experiences we learn the meaning of presence, and we formulate and fashion our prayer.

PRAYER AS SACRAMENT

To pray is to make the most of our moments of vision, of oneness, of beauty, of goodness, of pain. This "sacrament of prayer" is for me most eloquently spoken in George Bernanos's *Diary of a Country Priest*. A simple sentence on the lips of a dying man, gathering up all the fragments of his thankless and unrecognized ministry, of his most sordid human contacts. *Toute est grace:* all is grace. A lonely country road enveloped in the stark beauties of nature. The souls of sturdy peasant people, grappling with poverty and aching for human understanding. The rocky way from seminary training to the concrete, messy problems of sinful, saintly, people. The loneliness of a country priest, and the longing for union and fullness and happiness. *Toute est grace.*

At an ecumenical service of celebration and solidarity, the participants were asked to give the person next to them a gift, of a word or a blessing or a scripture verse. My neighbor, a young Lutheran from the United States, gave me those three words from Bernanos: All is grace. Sacrament of prayer. Outward sign of an inward grace. Moving me to find the meaning in this moment. Opening me to the layers of truth and beauty that lie beneath the surface of my surroundings. Daring me to probe the deeper side of pain and disappointment. Transforming the ordinary into mystery, and mystery into revelation.

Outward signs of inward transformations. Jesus was a master at pointing to such signs. Jesus and his followers moved in a sacramental milieu. And Jesus the teacher instructed the disciples in an incarnational spirituality. Do you know the sign of the barren fig tree? What is the message of the seed and the various soils? The storm on the lake was a sacrament, re-enkindling their faith. And the little child set in their midst was a sacramental sign of God's realm. The alabaster box of ointment, the widow's coin, the cup of cold water; all signs of an interior capacity and willingness to keep one's priorities aligned with those of the "blessed." The welcome and the honoring of the prodigal son mirrored the lavishness of divine mercy. The parable of the buried treasure signified the wholeheartedness and single-mindedness of this way. And the parable of the vineyard cautioned about human carelessness and infidelity.

As the time of Jesus' human life drew to an end, the sacramental signs became more poignant and more dramatic. Servant-leadership and hospitality will be forever associated with a towel and washbasin. The washing of feet authenticates the ritualizing and verbalizing of our liturgies and communion services. The shared cup and the broken bread become the lasting memorial of Jesus' total self-giving. Each time you do this, remember me. Remember what it means, the willingness to spend yourself for others.

When I was a child, my life was cluttered with certain symbols and signs of a simple faith, and of a yearning for identification with that state of mind we called sanctity and the realm we called heaven. I was a child of my times, and asceticism and personal holiness ranked high. I knelt daily in May before a crude altar, crowded with a statue of Mary and flowers snatched from our garden, as well as from the nearby Protestant cemetery. Lent meant penance. And penance meant two things: giving up candy, and praying the rosary on one's knees, leaning over a kitchen chair during the last good hours of daylight and fading hopes for an evening ball game. Christmas meant cribs, including angels and shepherds and camels. We even played "Mass," blasphemously placing bread-hosts on each other's tongues and prophetically permitting female priests.

For the most part, I have put away my childish ways. But sacraments, pointing the way to prayer and a life of mystery and grace, continue. What is it in your room that stretches beyond your intimate, personal world and leads you into the human streams of need? Perhaps a small gift given by someone you met in unusual circumstances or from another land, a picture that speaks to you, your scriptures, or a bookmark that regularly trips you up and re-evokes your commitment. It is for this same reason that we wear rings, and I wear a Tau cross. It is why we Catholics bury people with a rosary wrapped around their fingers. It is the purpose of sacred oils and Easter water and blessed ashes. It is the significance of rainbows and candles and incense.

Religious persons, I believe, gradually enlarge their vision and their sense of the sacred until most of their surroundings become a sign. There is a man who feels a special contact with his deceased father whenever he looks up at the stars. And my friend in Europe who sees mountains and vineyards and wanderwegs as personal parables. Why do we gather rocks from special places? And collect October leaves? Birthstones and grave-stones and diplomas and wedding cakes "hold" the meaning for us.

One of the sacraments of presence that is central to my life is the letter. Do you know anyone who doesn't cast a hopeful eye at the mailbox at a regular time every day? Surely you have waited impatiently for the answer about a job, the forgiving word, the promise of remembrance on an important occasion. No matter how technologically progressive we become, the letter remains the sacrament of exchange and of presence. I have precious letters written three months before my nephew died of liver cancer. It will be a present one day to his little daughter. I have a box full of letters written by a friend who has walked with me these last five years. I have saved letters from a seven-year-old niece who is now an adult. I also view letters that I send as gifts, gifts of my presence to those whom I love. I prefer letters to phone calls in ordinary circumstances because they can be savored, and taken out again and again to deepen the joy and the lived connection.

The letters of Bonhoeffer, written in prison, are tender gifts of presence. He wrote to his mother on her birthday, just four months before he was killed. He told her that he knew she shared all that he was going through. And he thanked her for the love she had brought into his cell the past year. "I feel myself so much a part of you all, that I know we live and bear everything in common, acting and thinking for one another even when we are separated."[5]

There are many holy moments in our daily lives. And one way we can capture and retain their significance is to gather them into a sign: a handclasp, a note, a tear, a word of affirmation, a blessing. Nothing need be lost. We learn to sacramentalize our walks, our work, our encounters, our routines. The seasons become rhythmic messages, places become hallowed, and events open up their secrets. There is more mystery and more meaning in the ordinary. Prayer becomes something natural and spontaneous, and bears the unique marks of our own imagery and our own style of communication.

PRAYER OF EXCHANGE

In prayer we become more like the "Other." It is in our many forms of prayer—meditation, liturgy, psalms, scripture reading—that we aim to come closer to the values and vision of Jesus and of the God who sent him. We try to immerse ourselves in the way of the gospel and in the style of God's loving. We "take on," as it were, the attitudes and priorities of Jesus. Our prayer, if genuine and persistent, transforms us into persons who more nearly resemble the God of our prayers.

Then our prayer spills over into living testimonies of that union and communion. We become the go-between. Prayer is not authentic until it has this transforming, dynamic effect. It leads to engagement and exchange. Merton put it thus: silence leads to compassion. We cannot prayerfully contemplate the scriptures without converting those words and admonitions into action and commitment. Similarly, we gain access to God by our love for human beings. They open us and "tender" us for that loving encounter that we call prayer. Dorothee Soelle says: "In every prayer an angel waits for us, since every prayer changes the one who prays, strengthens him [sic], in that it pulls him together and brings him to the utmost attention, forced from us in suffering, given by us in love."[6]

"No one who comes will I ever reject." Just as we are assured attention and mercy from God, so does it become more and more impossible for us to reject anyone who comes to us in need. "Whatever the Father (or Mother) does," Jesus says, "the Son does likewise." The resemblance is that great. And "All that God has belongs to me." The claim becomes that total.

Prayer identifies us with the "Other" and uncovers new modes of exchange. For example, prayer "conquers our heart." This is the converting power of prayer. There have been times in my life, all too many times, when I did not want to include a particular person in my prayers. I did not want to face my animosity and could not hold that person in a caring way. I have found that when I succeed in naming this person and praying for him or her over a period of time, there is a gradual softening of my stubborn and resistant heart. Peace finds a way to stretch between us and draw us into some kind of unity. I often wonder why we so seldom pray for those who are opposed to our dreams and priorities: the rulers of certain countries, those who are personal obstacles, those whom we have hurt. We tend to name all those with whom we already experience solidarity. Perhaps our hearts need to be conquered by a disciplined attention in prayer. Jesus explicitly bade us to pray for our enemies and to bless those who persecute us. He himself spoke the words: forgive them, for they know not what they do.

Additionally, prayer opens us to see with the eyes of Jesus and to become vulnerable and sensitive to other people, especially the "little ones" of our world. It is the grace whereby we begin to act like the "Other," to show mercy and concern, to identify with the poor and oppressed as did Jesus of Nazareth. Perhaps it is a leper experience of our own that wounds us, and links us with the outcasts and undesirables of our world. Perhaps it comes through the plea of an "illegal alien" that confirms our privileged status and birthright. The moving story of a missionary or even a television news clipping can evoke this moment of prayer. We move out of ourselves, enter another world, and begin to share the way of suffering or the burdens of others. We open the door and go out to the borders of our life.

Once we really absorb ourselves with those in need, life will never again be the same. The details of our life will begin to be affected, the friends we have and lose, the form of security we seek, the work we choose or choose not to do. All things in life start to connect and to direct us toward further conversion.

For me the race riots and the peace demonstrations of the sixties cracked into my cloistered, sheltered life. Then it was the sights and smells of India, the faces of the men and women lined up at Ben's meal program, the burned body of a little boy from North Dakota, the vacant look of a student in a mental hospital, my drug-prone niece. Aware of our limitations, we find some energy to reach out, to take residence even briefly in another's world, to utter a word of respect, to lift a hand in a compassionate gesture, or simply to stand in silence with another. "We are most deeply asleep at the switch when we fancy we control any switches at all." If we understand, it will be because we've been silent "before the deepening wonder of Christ."[7]

Our prayer of intercession becomes a prayer of exchange as well as of presence. It is more than petition. To intercede means to plead the case of, to step in on behalf of someone. I tend to think that if we take this prayer seriously we must be willing to lay something of ourselves on the line. We must be willing to offer something, in the manner of Charles Williams's theory of substitution. We pray and we love in a way that gives something, takes something of the other's burden, exchanges places, however mysteriously and limitedly. My sister-in-law, for example, who faces terminal cancer, offers her pain for blessing on my and others' mission. Her cancer becomes fruitful as she substitutes concern for others for self-pity. William Stringfellow writes: "The one who intercedes for another is confessing that his or her trust in the vitality of the Word of God is so serious that he or she volunteers risks, sharing the burden of the one for whom intercession is offered even to the extremity of taking the place of the other person who is the subject of the prayer."[8] In *Life Together*, Bonhoeffer says that "intercessory prayer is the purifying bath into which the individual and the community must enter every day."[9] It is purifying because it strips us of our illusions about our self-sufficiency. It reminds us of the kinship we share with persons of every way of life and with all manner of human need.

This is the intent of the ecumenical prayer circle, this linking of hearts and lives around the globe and across every line of confession and geography. We pray this week for the people of Chile, Peru, and Bolivia. We all attend to their needs and stand for an "eternal moment" in their place. We celebrate their gifts and intercede for their concerns. And if we do this in truth, we never quite return those people to oblivion. They have affected us in some real way, and we must allow that to find expression in our local and personal lives. It is prayer of intercession that makes explicit the possibility of exchange that is always there. It makes us conscious of the ways we are linked and bound to one another. It calls us to offer something of ourselves so that the cares of another may be relieved. It reveals the almost visible, tangible, life of the Spirit that goes between us.

It was my forty-seventh birthday, and I was in Raisen, India. Word came to me that someone from London was trying to get through by phone. I emphasize trying. With a friend I went some distance to the local police station to await the possible call, since they had better phone lines. The entire force got involved. It was no insignificant event, a London call coming to this little market town in central India. Surely it was some important communication. I sat on a stool and listened to the police bustling about, shouting in Hindi to one another, and carefully keeping the line open so that this mysterious caller would have access. Eventually I had to give up. The call got as far as Bhopal, about fifty kilometers away. But the local system was not efficient enough to relay it. All the time, of course, I knew who it was and why it was coming. In fact I was wondering what I would say if it did come, with the police staff listening in and expecting important news. Though I never heard my friend's voice, I felt her presence nonetheless. We were connected in an awesome way. Her message filled the air in that part of India. My heart resonated: We were in touch. She, too, had sat near the phone for hours, waiting to see if London could reach Raisen. It was prayer, if prayer is closing the gaps of time and distance.

Prayer and presence are, by their nature, forms of exchange and connectedness. We can block the flow of life and movement. We can respond to the invitation to enter the dynamic. "Two men went up to the temple to pray: one was a Pharisee, the other a tax collector." (Luke 18:9) One prayed about himself, not even for himself. His was a prayer of complacency. The other beat his breast and confessed his sins, the injuries he had inflicted on other human beings. The lack of other-directedness is a block to the prayer of exchange. By our self-preoccupation we cut off the healing, energizing life that could spill over to others.

"I have kept all the commandments since I was a youth." (Luke 18:18) The rich young man wanted to know the way into the life of exchange, but he was not willing to pay the price, to offer "substitution" as his entry into the mystery. He held on to what he could have given and blocked the exchange of gifts. He had no needs, and failed to realize that his greatest need was to be in need. We choke life by our possessiveness and exclusive claims to gifts that are meant to be shared.

"Teacher, grant our request. See to it that we sit one at your right, and the other at your left, when you come into your glory." (Mark 10:35) You don't know what you are asking, Jesus told them. Sometimes our prayer has little to do with the new world we say we want to help build. We are blind and we miss the clues. Instead of participating in the process of liberation and justice, we fall into the false ways of ambition and greed. Our narrow perspectives limit the life we could enlarge.

The call to prayer and presence is an invitation to sacramentalize our lives. To see God's prints and traces in the world about us. To be constantly surprised by sacred codes revealed in nature. To use all the creative powers available, of gesture, and language, and every manner of human communication. To increase the "life" of prayer through music and art and symbol.

It is an invitation to travel from our worship into our wider world of contacts, and from that context back into worship, until our love has expanded and deepened, and our prayer transforms us into"gentle presences." The transition from prayer to action can become less and less noticeable. Our prayer over Jerusalem and our action on behalf of Jerusalem become one effort. It is an invitation to strike the rock, to become a site where the Holy Spirit acts, where life and power can flow out into other lives and into the concrete affairs of human beings. "We will come to you and make our dwelling place with you." (John 14:23) "When the Spirit of truth comes, you will be guided to all truth." (John 16:13)

SEVEN

HOPE AND TRANSFORMATION

"The people here have to do lots for themselves and they do. It's the idea of forming basic communities of people who share faith and life. It's a slow process, but it's working. It's a little sign of hope. . . .These young women want to be about service to the folks who crave to hear the Word of God. They give me so much hope for the future of our community."

"They cut me down and I leap up high. I am the life that'll never die. I'll live in you if you'll live in me. I am the Lord of the dance, said he."[1]   The dance continues, in its eternal rhythms and flow. Living and dying, dying and rising, ending and beginning. The cycles and circles of our co-inherence with one another, with all that is and was and will be.

We hope because Jesus has "moved in with us"[2] and turned reality upside down, opened a new vision for us, the mystery and miracle of our unity. Jesus has demonstrated that the resurrection is here and now, as well as a promise. That for every death there is the possibility of new life. That creation and the exodus and the coming of God's realm are happening in our midst. And that nothing happens that is not part of all that happens.

How many times have we stood huddled together at a funeral service and renewed our hope in life and in the lasting imprint of a human existence, even as we tearfully spoke our fare-wells? We are the hope that the presence and the witness of this beloved person will endure. We are the fruit of his or her dying, for our life is renewed even as we accept our loss. We re-commit ourselves to the human bonds of community and to a life of exchange. Why is death a time for hope? Perhaps it is our human need to immortalize, to keep alive the song the beloved sang and the dreams he or she envisioned. Perhaps it is a time when we actually stop and peer into the mystery of human exis-tence and its meaning. At that moment we confront our own mor-tality and we feel an urgency rising within us, to hold life carefully, but to spend it lavishly on things that matter. It is perhaps one time when "we have the experience" and don't "miss the meaning."[3]

Anniversaries—of foundings, of fidelities, of heroic deeds—are also a time for hope. It is our human urge to remem-ber, to hear the songs we once sang and to reconstruct the dreams we dreamed. It is a time when we stop and gaze backward at the mystery of life intertwined. It is a time when we give thanks and gather the fragments and go forth into the next un-known with new awarenesses and new resolution.

Hope lives, it seems, on that brink between the near and the far, the finite and the infinite, the now and the not-yet. It is our human power of bridging what is yet humanly unbridged, of believing what is not yet seen, of seeing what is not yet visi-ble. In Dan Berrigan's words, it is "living as though the truth were true."[4] When told of the limits of our life or of others, we hope. When faced with separations and severings, we hope. When confronted by obstacles and impasses and trials of all sorts, we hope. Outwardly all seems lost or fraught with pain or without meaning. But hope reveals in that very reality a hidden meaning. Perhaps it can't be named, but it exists. It is hope that sifts through the diverse contents of life's deliveries and finds the good news.

St. Paul tells the tale of hope in his letter to the Romans: "I consider the sufferings of the present to be as nothing compared with the glory to be revealed in us. Indeed, the whole created world awaits the revelation of the children of God...the world itself will be freed from its slavery to corruption and share in the glorious freedom of the children of God. Yes, we know that all creation groans and is in agony, even until now. Not only that, but we ourselves, although we have the Spirit as first fruits, groan inwardly while we await the redemption of our bodies. In hope we were saved. But hope is not hope if its object is seen; how is it possible for one to hope for what one sees? And hoping for what we cannot see means awaiting it with patient endurance. . . .We know that God makes all things work together for the good of those who love. . . . (8:18-28)

That tale has been echoed in the previous chapters of this book. That tale repeats itself in your life and in mine, in human endurance and in our capacity for renewal. The human story is a narrative of hope. The birth of a child is a sign of God's continued hope in us as a people. The death of each person arouses an awareness of the meaning of life and our potential for making it more abundant for all. We wait for healing and for forgiveness. We pray in hope. Love waits in trembling hope for its outcome. In hope we move in solidarity between new emerging communities and the wrecked communities of the displaced. In hope we suffer and are transformed by the flow and forces of life.

In this final chapter we go to the borders of our "slavery to corruption" and we peer into 1) the "glorious freedom" that is ours; we wait in anticipation, 2) while "creation groans and is in agony," and 3) we affirm that "all things work together" for those who love and who hope.

GLORIOUS FREEDOM

In various ways in the preceding pages, we have seen the depths and the scope of creation's agony. The tensions on all levels, the strains placed on human beings, the hostilities and the chasms, the misplaced priorities and the ignored needs. So-called free countries contradict themselves with their manifold discriminations, materialistic standards, and their ease in imposing ideologies and life styles on others. So-called free people endure their treadmill existences, exhaust themselves in competition, and remain indifferent to the plight of others. Our lives are marked by that futility of which St. Paul speaks. What difference will it make if I do something? The needs are too vast. The obstacles are insurmountable. It is too late.

Hope is a scarce commodity even in Christian circles. The weight and the threatening nature of the world's problems paralyze us or send us scampering back to our quiet, comfortable enclaves for consolation and relief. Hope is a small word in a giant cosmos on the edge of disaster. We look around at all the Goliaths and we smile patronizingly at the handful of Davids lifting their hopeful slings. Hope somehow must mean hope in oneself, and it is obvious that the mightiest efforts of a single person will not suffice to dent the armor of the powers we face. Dare we hope in one another? We have grave doubts. Our experiences of human cooperation are feeble and disappointing. Hope in God, in the Spirit alive and active in our midst? What does that mean? Isn't it clear that we've made the mess and we're on our own and that time is running out? Hope is but a faint flicker, a last remaining and isolated coal. A word we tuck into our prayers, between faith and charity.

Of course we long to be free, to share in the glorious freedom of the children of God. But we aren't naive. We are realistic. We live in the here and now. We've been cured, many of us, by those lonely marches in the cold rain, or by our futile knocking at the doors of magistrates, of our romantic illusions about social change and action for justice. We've been disillusioned as even more conservative governments come into power. Summit meetings fail, famine and the poor distribution of resources claim more and more lives. Even our attempts to live alternatively have turned a bit sour. Co-ops and alliances have gone the way of less well-intentioned mergers, broken by human conflict, rendered ineffective by internal struggles for leadership, caught in their inability to adapt and to find creative approaches. Peace groups, consciousness-raising groups, action groups of all sorts become tired and discouraged. Membership dwindles, a few carry the burdens, funds and imagination run out. What is this glorious Christian freedom? Christians seem so smug, so apathetic, so concerned about their own schools, their own renewal programs, their own balanced budgets. Fringe groups continue of course, without any religious labels, and occasionally we join them. But the staying power, the commitment, the enthusiasm, are gone. Hope for a better world barely trickles in our veins.

Is it because the stakes are so much higher these days? Is it because arrest and jail are inevitable consequences? Divestment means loss. Rebellion against authority draws severe punishment. Economic sharing and an option for the poor entail substantial changes in our way of life. Reconciliation and the willingness to convert mean letting go of pride and of old self-images. Even refusing to fit into roles, to read prepared scripts, has a price tag. Constructive plans are far more demanding than impulsive reactions. Making choices requires reflection and determination. Accepting the status quo is easier. Are we really ready to plunge into the streams of struggle? It is easier to talk about it and approve of others' involvement. Are we even ready to expose our views when our reputation, the approval of others, a possible promotion, are endangered? Is it not true that many of us have half-decided to live our lives in expediency, even if that means reducing large areas of our lives to trivia? "There is always an enormous temptation to diddle around making itsy-bitsy friends and meals and journeys for itsy-bitsy years on end." We don't, Annie Dillard chides, "go up into the gaps."[5] We don't walk fearlessly, unfurling our vision of vastness. Justice and freedom from all manner of oppression are not live coals in our breasts impelling us into the maelstrom.

We forget we are on a journey, that "seventy is the sum of our years, or eighty if we are strong." (Psalm 90:10) We lose sight of our condition as pilgrims and nomads. We forget that we are all in exodus and that that is our glorious freedom; to be freed of the captivities that we have allowed and the complicities that we have engaged in. We forget that the seed of God is in us, and that, in Meister Eckhart's words, the seed of God grows into God, as a hazel seed grows into a hazel tree. We settle in and settle down. We grow complacent and lead practical lives.

And so our days become more and more trivial. We get caught in a hectic maze. Rising when the clock determines. Battered by news headlines that seem remote and beyond our influence. Jangled by all the mechanical operations that launch us into activity and productivity. Tested by traffic, forced to calculate time and distance to the second. Elevators and phones and gadgets guide us through necessary interactions and keep human interactions superficial and at a minimum. Our concentration is interspersed by meetings and small crises. At the end of the day we rewind ourselves: traffic, automation, headlines, until we set that alarm clock to dictate tomorrow's awakening. Routines of ticking and timing. Little room for responding humanly and humanely to the day's events; little time to enter into the wisdom and freshness and the promise of its opportunities. We feel our lives closing in, confining and conforming us.

Even times of prayer and worship become trivialized. We arrive breathless and use the anonymity of the service to unwrap our day's wares and file our future engagements. We are distracted by page numbers and the order of procession. We recite mechanically and listen half-heartedly. We speak a language foreign to that of common discourse, addressing a remote God. We approach the table without thought of the commitment our action signifies. We leave the church or time of prayer as we leave any other of our occupations, with a shrug and a sigh of relief. The experience has been a flight from prayer and from the simple sacredness of our lives. We have missed the experience of awe and reverence. We have failed to participate in the mysterious exchange that prayer offers. We have reinforced our lackluster, frenetic existence rather than advanced into our glorious freedom as children of God.

We become immune to the grandeur and glory of creation itself. We barely notice the cloud passing over the moon or the dewdrops clinging to the rose leaves. The ice on the pond comes and goes. The wild blackberries ripen and wither. The blackbird nests again outside our bedroom window. We don't see them. We avoid the cold and the heat. We screen our windows and entomb ourselves in plastic in winter. We fence off our properties. We eliminate weeds even when they have individual names and blossoms. We rake up every leaf as fast as it falls. We are so accustomed to buying food in supermarkets, and pre-packaged meat and fish, that we hardly think about how it grows or whence and how it came to us.

We walk amid nature's beauty and bounty and we talk non-stop. We miss the panorama of color and sound and smell. We could have remained in our closed, artificially lit, living rooms. Nature's lessons are lost, and the opportunity to be silent before the God of creation. We fail to be stretched by the magnificence and power of creation. It doesn't calm our tortured spirits, strengthen our dwindling reserves, restore our perspective, delight us in every part of our being. It reminds us instead of mundane chores: changing calendar pages, ordering our snow tires.

Our capacity for hope diminishes when there is no room for miracle or mystery. Our pragmatic mindsets have convinced us that most of the situations we find ourselves in are humanly solvable problems. Problems for UN agencies or for parliament. Problems of racism and urban decay. Problems of crime and mental illness. Domestic and personal problems. Even problems of church unity and dialogue. Those same mindsets reduce peace and justice, the dignity of persons, the interrelatedness of the human community, sin and evil, to tasks to be tackled and issues for research and theology.

In the midst of our long-range objectives, scientific formulas and periodic reviews, there is little atmosphere for hope. Hope belongs to the realm of the unsolvable, the ongoing mystery, the human endeavor to penetrate the darkness and obscurity of the reality that surrounds us. Love and truth, suffering and death, are realities that we are involved in, not objective problems we confront. We are developed by them as we experience them. We are in them, not outside them. They transcend us, compel us to explore a larger world of interaction and exchange.

The good news of our Christian faith is that our lives are

not trivia or defined by the problems we face. We are marked for glory, for freedom. "You are a letter of Christ written not with ink but by the Spirit of the living God...we are earthen vessels bearing a treasure...we carry about in our bodies the dying of Jesus, so that in our bodies the life of Jesus may be revealed." (2 Corinthians 3:6; 4:7,10-11) The gospel summons us into a world of courageous discipleship, of bold commitment, of active faith. It is no trivial task, no slight challenge. To give an account of the hope that is in us. In the midst of overwhelming poverty. In the face of killing cancer. Within the limits of a defensive church. Through grief and insult and loneliness. Speaking truth forcefully and without malice. Restructuring our priorities and making credible our value system. Plodding patiently through daily tasks and commitments. We are called to release life and meaning from all the secret and dim events of our personal and communal histories.

On some given day we become conscious, says Chardin, of the divine spread everywhere about us: a new sense, a transformation, in the very perception of being.[6] We look at a landscape and see an eternal beauty. We look at a human face and see the profile of dignity. Through every reality there shines a light, a grace, a glory. We are called to probe the forbidden, to unmask monsters, to look death in the eye. Called to love in love's inimitable way, by service and sacrifice and substitution. Our spirits may be weak, our bodies tired, our hopes may be faded. But we hunger still for good news. We yearn for redemption.

ALL CREATION GROANS
As I have written these pages, I have been surrounded by the silent activity of garden and field. The slow unfolding of buds and the unseen ripening of potatoes. The fullness of wheat fields and the bounty of apple orchards. Now it is harvest time and the silence is replaced by farm machines, carefully combing the growth, gathering the fruits, stacking the hay, picking and cutting and hauling. Autumn has arrived. The hopes of the planting season have been fulfilled. The long process of waiting has ended. It is not so everywhere, we know. But the seasons

and cycles of creation are everywhere constant cause for hope.

In human terms the growth and harvest are less clear. The groping, searching, waiting, gathering, follow no sure patterns and have no predictable outcomes. Food doesn't reach those most in need. No cure has been found for lung cancer or for AIDS. Hostages live in terror and suspense. We fight against our addictions and prejudices. Innocent children are the pawns of governments and ruthless extremists. The agony of the world is written in human souls and on human faces. As hope dawns in one part of the world, shadows cover another. "Drawn to our human scale, the world appears as an immense groping in the dark, an immense searching, an immense onslaught, wherein there can be no advance save at the cost of many setbacks and many wounds. Those who suffer, whatever form their suffering may take, are a living statement of this austere but noble condition: they are simply paying for the advance and the victory of all."[7]

We live in a paradox. We live flawed lives. Our creative imaginations are child-size in an adult-sized world. With weak faith we grope through the influx of global issues and immediate agendas. Our hope is so small. We turn, in our bewilderment and our uncertainty, to something sure, to God's Word. When that Word enters a vulnerable place in our spirits, we are not cured of our restlessness and our discomfort. We are jolted perhaps out of our cleverness and our sophistry. We begin to be carved out, a passageway for a message that will not leave us in peace. We begin to transmit something vital to others, something of ourselves, of the meaning the Word holds for us. Our spiritual ideals and our real lives become entangled. Our wounds, our discouragements, our mistakes, become part of the currency of a new exchange. Our hope buds into a living experience.

Jeopardized health. The strain of love. Conflicts in community. Costly freedoms. The Word addresses each of them. We are more like one another than alone. We are one with the victims and the makers of history. We still wince under the throb of our personal wounds. We still feel the burden of the oppressions that beset us. But we review our blessings. We sense how connected are our sorrows and our joys. We are part of that stream of believers who see but dimly where faith leads them.

That hope, as it springs, leads to testimony. Wounds are to be shared, their fruits multiplied. The nourishing Word is to be broken, and distributed. The haunting messages are to be companions directing us and others onto paths we don't recognize and into places from which we naturally shrink. The Word that pierced and now prods must be preached. Preached by practice, by prophetic actions, in making happen here and now what yet remains a hope and a promise. We are pressed more deeply into the patterns of exchange, into conversion and transformation, and into a wider vision of a world renewed. Daily, repeatedly, that Word, its paradox, its peril, its promise, takes root, sprouts, grows, and produces.

The flames of Soweto, the anguish of division, the misery and poverty of the landless seared Desmond Tutu's being. Wounded by the realities of injustice and apartheid, he has become a sign of contradiction. He has passed through fear and the stings of recrimination. His word and his priesthood and his actions are woven into one piece. Now to all who will listen, he can stand boldly in the midst of the conflict. He is free to be pastor of black and white in Capetown. The truth has set him free.

I know a fragile woman, now in her seventies, to whom life has dealt blow upon blow. Her only brother, her sole family, was diagnosed as mad. She stayed at his side until he died. Only then it was discovered that he had a brain tumor. She herself lost a breast to cancer. She never married. She loved a man in silence for years on end, not interfering with his marriage. After forty years of waiting and testing, his wife died. Perhaps at last. But the man mysteriously committed suicide. A final blow. Yet, people now come to this woman as an oasis. She has kept all these things in her wounded heart, pondering them. "Happy those whose strength you are! When they pass through the bitter valley, they make it a place of springs." (Psalm 84:6-7)

We drove south to London into the green, wooded beauty of

Hampshire. Suddenly we came upon the desert. Barren fields of cement and camouflaged training sites, stretch upon stretch of barbed wire. The Greenham Common Base has a number of entrances and at several of them a small group of women keep camp. For years women have kept vigil, a small circle of human hope around a destructive center. Dramatic moments occur: eviction and abuse, arrests and prison. There is the slow, steady attrition of energies from rain and cold and fatigue. But the women remain. New recruits come. Theirs is a relentless belief. Evil is in our midst, procreating death and despair. The growth of the arms market depends on public acceptance of bases like this. But there is another vision, of a saner, safer world, and it depends on signs, of human interaction, and endurance in the protest. The reign of God is also in our midst.

We are never too old or too weak to begin cultivating the fruit that lasts. At age fifty-five a women looks back over her childless life. She was a missionary for a large portion of her life, planting seeds of confidence and leadership through her education work in East Africa. She helped Asian Ugandans find new homes and futures in another land. She worked with churches and their role in race relations. She endeavored for nine years to use her position internationally to promote an exchange of resources and to be a catalyst for the renewal of congregations and communities. Her conviction grew that plowing and planting were needed in the heart of the church body, at the local level. Wounded by the words, "the harvest is rich, but the laborers are scarce," she gave up her salaried and safe position to enter a life of risk and uncertainty in that cause. The way of the grain of wheat is the way to fruit that remains.

I was introduced to Doris by a mutual friend in Ben's community. She was recovering from depression and temporarily homeless. She felt at ease and accepted among the "wild life" members of this inner-city sanctuary. A few weeks later she introduced me to Walter, a man from the streets whom she had recruited. Both looked cheerful and kempt. A Sunday or so later she introduced me to still another friend, Bill, who admitted he'd never before darkened the door of a church. I felt the ripple of community growing and saw changes in Doris's appearance and expression. Then one day Doris left her seat at the end of the service and with obvious pride and self-assurance she stood at the door distributing the church announcements. She was now the gate through which others were finding the green pastures of acceptance and self-worth. It was only a moment in the search and vision of a community, but it was "washing each other's feet" in the manner of Jesus.

As I stood in the hot sun in the village of Barla in Central India, I felt I was at the ends of the earth. The brown bodies of the villagers glistened with sweat as, in relay teams, they carried rock and soil from the widening hole. A well-digging was in progress. Occasionally they sang and often there was laughter. Prayers to their Hindu gods, respect for the Roman Catholic sisters who had spearheaded the project, complete trust that water would be found. They were doing what their ancestors had done, in the way they had done it. They understood the value and the meaning of water. I saw how pervasive the sense of God was in this remote, starkly poor village. And I knew: "I am with you always until the end of the world."

The words of the gospel have found a home in our world if we have eyes to see and hearts to believe. There are reasons for hope, and seeds of hope which are ours to tend. As a Zen saying puts it: no seed ever sees the flower. But the flower can't come unless the seed is planted. "Let us plant dates even though those who plant them will never eat them. We must live by the love of what we will never see. . . .Such disciplined love is what has given prophets, revolutionaries, and saints the courage to die for the future they envisaged. They make their own bodies the seed of their highest hope."[8]

ALL THINGS WORK TOGETHER

A friend and I were driving in the city, headed for a shopping mall, when without warning there was a loud noise and the car stopped. Not a spark of life. Our plans for the day changed just as abruptly. We discovered that a bolt had loosened and the motor had actually slipped, disconnecting itself from the fuel pipe. In two days we would have been airport-bound for my flight to Europe. Our repeated exclamation in the aftermath of the trouble was: "Thank God it happened today!" The inconvenience and expense seemed minor in relation to what could have happened.

We learn, slowly and reluctantly, that it is pain that gives importance, especially in human affairs. When we lose something, we have a new appreciation of its value. When security is threatened, we realize how complacent we have been. When doubts arise, or disagreements separate us, we cherish anew the wholeness and peace of harmonious relationships. We have to harden our hearts, says Robinson Jeffers, to bear humility's beauty, for it is impure and often painful.[9] Gibran speaks of the same paradox: "When you are joyous, look deep into your heart and you shall find it is only that which has given you sorrow that is giving you joy. When you are sorrowful, look again in your heart, and you shall see that in truth you are weeping for that which has been your delight."[10] The promise cannot be separated from the pain. The potential reality is contained within actual darkness. We have to become more than we presently are when we exercise hope. We have to become as strong as the storms we head into, and as large as the circles we reach out to embrace.

Hope has two daughters, it is said: anger and courage. It is they who enable us to make happen what we want to happen in the future. Anger and courage lead us to snip fences at military bases, to sit in at offices of elected officials. They lead us to treat as our equals and as brothers and sisters the deportable aliens, the slum residents, the homosexuals, the men and women in our jails. They lead us to beg bread at the communion tables of our churches. They lead us to turn upside down the hierarchical systems, the male-dominated structures, the class-conscious conventions, the clerical mentalities, the success syndromes. They lead us to transform, by tiny deliberate efforts, the priorities and preoccupations of our personal lives and to believe in the transformation of society even while nothing seems to improve or change.

Transubstantiation is a sacrament. Whether it is food prepared for the homeless, our fears turning into freedoms, our bodies put on the line for justice and peace. It has other names: conversion, renewal, kenosis, solidarity, hope. What is before us, what appears to be impenetrable and anti-life, can become moist and fertile. We live in that expectation. "The secret of life is to act as though we already possessed the thing we most painfully lack. . . .To convince ourselves that everything is created for good...for if I believe it, and you, and everyone, it will become real."[11]

When hope is allowed a chance, it works secretly and in small ways. The dough rises and becomes bread. You can't force the process. Tiny grains planted deep in the furrowed earth become a vast field of sugar beets or barley. No use trying to hurry it. The heart of hope is an attentive patience. Patience is greatly misunderstood. When I waited in that mental ward many years ago, something was happening, slowly and imperceptibly. When another line of resisters is dragged off to the bailiff, something is happening. When communities gather day in and day out to reflect and discern together, something is happening. We are living the questions, in Rilke's words. Much in our hearts and our world is unsolved. We are not capable of many of the answers, and perhaps not ready to pay the price. "Live the questions now. Perhaps you will then gradually, without noticing it, live along some distant day into the answer."[12]

My mother used to say to me, in countless circumstances in my childhood: Wait and see. I often interpreted it to mean: Don't hope too much, prepare yourself to give it up, be resigned to your disappointment. Occasionally by the inflection in her voice and the twinkle in her eye, I knew it meant: I'm not certain, but I fully expect that your wish will be granted. As Christians, we have lost much of our sense of expectancy. The noise and rush of Christmas crowd out any Advent sense of hope. We associate waiting with inactivity and resignation. We pass through events in our life, we move from mountain to mountain, getting through the valleys with as much dispatch as possible. We have forgotten the art of anticipation. Our hope lacks passion and energy. We no longer expect anything of ourselves, of our leaders, of our combined efforts and power. We are not enthusiastic about any good news. We are not captured and enlivened by small signs of hope. We are serious and somber and terribly literal about most of life. We don't believe that the Spirit is completely free to creatively transform us and what is taking place just beyond our gaze. We aren't radical in our faith. We don't fix our hearts on the one thing necessary. We don't believe in signs. We still seek saviors.

Hope does not emanate from us. We are lax and lazy in our celebrating. Our prayer styles and our times of worship lack imagination and festivity. We are hesitant and wary in our trusting. We place so much emphasis on our own words and our own planning. We fail to listen to the whispers of God's action and to see the imprints of the Spirit's influence. We are niggardly in our role as reconcilers. We demand overtures from one another, we wait upon our self-righteousness. We refuse the limited offering while we continue to inflict our threats. Our faces are stony and often blank. We carry gloom in our bodies and gestures. People aren't curious about us. "Who is this man?" asked so many people who met Jesus. He clearly had a secret which attracted and puzzled. We fit into the background, we stir up no controversy, we represent no threat. We are not caught by the contagious spirit of the true disciples, the revolutionaries, the prophets, the saints of our day.

It is autumn. Mists hang in the morning over trees turning golden and orange. Fields have been flattened. A harvest moon lights up the crisp September skies. A time to be attentive to signs. The trees will soon surrender their foliage. Plowed fields will store the seeds during winter's freeze. Hours of daylight and darkness will shift. As I walked today, I noticed a surviving poppy bobbing atop a junk heap.

Dotted across your landscape and mine are signs, of new beginnings, of necessary deaths. Ominous signs, casting shadows over life's fullness and potential. Bomber pilots training overhead. Terrorist victims in Paris and Karachi. Continued silence from a discouraged and disappointed friend. And there are gospel signs, tiny beacons of light and hope. Communities of reconciliation in Ireland, renewed peace efforts requested by the bishop of El Salvador. A widower in his loneliness and grief rebuilds his life by selfless service among the villagers. A dying woman cheers her visitors with her unquenchable humor. Our hearts are vigilant. Too long have we had the experience and missed the meaning. "I think it would be well, and proper, and pure, to grasp your own necessity and not let it go, to dangle from it limp wherever it takes you."[13]

What body will we give our hope? How and when will we live our visions? Hope is not a distant dream. Hope is here, nudging us to resist, to celebrate, to trust, to reconcile, to do that which will make real what our heart treasures. If faith is a mustard seed and love is a crossbar, then hope is a flame. The light shines in the darkness, and the darkness cannot extinguish it. It is an eternal flame. It draws on the vast deep fuel of the human spirit, a spirit receptive to the divine touch.

I remember hearing a comparison between the Indian style of coping with the cold and the habits of Caucasians. Indians build a small fire and gather close around it. Caucasians build a huge fire and stand back. Let us grasp the lesson and gather close in a circle, in many circles that intersect. There is a time for despair, but not now. There is a time for resignation, but not now. There is a time for waiting, but not now. This is a time for joining hands and drawing close to that central flame, for warmth and encouragement. The dance is in progress. All of creation groans to be released into its motion. Human hands and hearts are extended, awaiting a response. We are a link in the circle. We are the hope that the witness of our martyrs and prophets will endure. We are the fruit of their dying. We recommit ourselves to the human bonds of community and to a life of exchange.

ENDNOTES

INTRODUCTION

1. Joan Puls, O.S.F., *Every Bush Is Burning*, (Mystic, Connecticut: Twenty-Third Publications, 1986), 88.

CHAPTER ONE

1. The passages that open each chapter are excerpts from letters, which are one concrete form of personal exchange. The passages chosen were trigger, inspiration, and part of the wrestling for the reflections that follow.

2. The forced displacement of Africans and the history of slavery is another tale.

3. Annie Dillard, *Teaching a Stone to Talk*, (New York: Harper & Row, 1982), 70.

4. T.S. Eliot, *Four Quartets*, (London: Faber and Faber, 1940), 20.

5. McNeill, Morrison, Nouwen, *Compassion*, (New York: Doubleday and Company, Inc., 1982), 72.

6. T.S. Eliot, *Four Quartets*, 8.

7. Ibid.

8. Thomas Merton, *Asian Journal*, (New York: New Directions Books, 1975), 305.

9. Dorothy Day, *The Long Loneliness*, (San Francisco: Harper & Row, 1952), 214.

10. Simone Weil, *The Simone Weil Reader*, (New York: David McKay Co., Inc., 1977), xxxii.

11. Vincent Donovan, *Christianity Rediscovered*, (Maryknoll, New York: Orbis Books, 1983), 193.

12. W.H. Vanstone, *Love's Endeavour, Love's Expense*, (London: Darton, Longman and Todd, 1977), 52.

13. Teilhard de Chardin, *The Divine Milieu*, (New York: Harper & Row, 1960), 89-90.

14. T.S. Eliot, *Four Quartets*, 20.

15. *Epistle to Diognetus*, 2nd century.

16. Annie Dillard, *Holy the Firm*, (New York: Harper & Row, 1977), 56-7.

CHAPTER TWO

1. J.V. Taylor, *Weep Not for Me*, (Mystic, Connecticut: Twenty-Third Publications, 1986), 15.

2. William Blake, *Selected Poems*, (London: Oxford University Press, 1951), 41.

3. J.V. Taylor, *Weep Not for Me*, 19.

4. Ibid., 33.

5. Charles Williams, *Seed of Adam*, (London: Oxford University Press, 1948), 11.

6. Mary McDermott Shideler, *The Theology of Romantic Love* (New York: Harper & Row, 1962), 24.

7. Thomas Merton, *Asian Journal*, 157-8.

8. Charles Williams, *He Came Down from Heaven*, (London: Faber and Faber, 1950), 86.

9. Dietrich Bonhoeffer, *Letters and Papers from Prison*, (New York: The Macmillan Company, 1967), 150.

10. C.S. Lewis, *Four Loves*, (New York: Harcourt, Brace, Jovanovich, Inc., 1960), 111-12.

11. Teilhard de Chardin, *The Divine Milieu*, 143-4.

12. Lao Tzu, from *Peacemaking: Day by Day* (Pax Christi), (Erie, Pennsylvania: Benet Press), 110.

13. Charles Williams, *He Came Down from Heaven*, 82ff.

14. Julian of Norwich, *Revelations of Divine Love*, (New York: Penguin Books, 1966), 185.

15. Kahlil Gibran, *The Prophet*, (New York: Alfred A. Knopf, 1923), 11-12.

16. T.S. Elliot, *Four Quartets*, 42.

17. Radindranath Tagore, *Gitanjali*, (London: Macmillan and Co., Ltd., 1962), 46.

18. Bette Midler, "The Rose."

19. Kahlil Gibran, *The Prophet*, 13.

20. T.S. Eliot, *Four Quartets*, 44.

21. Rabindranath Tagore, *Gitanjali*, 46.

22. Bette Midler, "The Rose."

23. W.H. Vanstone, *Love's Endeavour, Love's Expense*, 115.

24. Simone Weil, *The Simone Weil Reader*, 370.

25. Fyodor Dostoevsky, *Brothers Karamazov*, often quoted by Dorothy Day.

26. Gabriel Marcel, *Being and Having*, (New York: Harper & Row, 1965), 47.

27. Rosemary Haughton, *The Passionate God*, (London: Darton, Longman and Todd, 1981), 91.

28. Anne Morrow Lindbergh, *Gift from the Sea*, (New York: Vintage Books, 1965), 104.

29. Helen Luke, *Dark Wood to White Rose*, (Pecos, New Mexico: Dove Publications, 1975), 141.

30. W.H. Vanstone, *Love's Endeavour, Love's Expense*, 120.

CHAPTER THREE

1. Annie Dillard, *Teaching a Stone to Talk*, 128.

2. Wendell Berry, *The Unsettling of America: Culture and Agriculture*, (Avon Books, 1977), 123.

3. Martin Buber, *I and Thou*, trans. Ronald Gregor Smith, (New York: Scribner, 1958), 94.

4. Vincent Donovan, *Christianity Rediscovered*, 187.

5. Ibid., 85-6.

6. Rosemary Haughton, "There Is Hope For a Tree," unpublished paper.

7. Andrew Hake, Anglican priest, in conversation.

8. Rosemary Haughton, "There Is Hope For a Tree," 8.

9. Lesslie Newbigin, *Foolishness to the Greeks*, (Geneva: World Council of Churches, 1986), 3-4.

10. Ibid., 15-19.

11. Ram Dass, *Grist for the Mill*, quoted in *Peacemaking: Day by Day*, 16.

CHAPTER FOUR

1. Helen Luke, *Dark Wood to White Rose*, 22.

2. Charles Williams, *He Came Down from Heaven*, 60.

3. W.H. Auden, *Age of Anxiety*, (New York: Random House, 1947), 134.

4. Jonathan Graham, *He Came unto His Own*, (London: Church Union, Church Literature Association, 1957), 53.

5. Letter of Ben and Carol Weir to friends and supporters.

6. J.V. Taylor, *Man in the Midst*, (London: CMS Highway Press, 1956), 53.

7. John Davies, *Beginning Now*, (London: Collins, 1971), 200.

CHAPTER FIVE

1. Teilhard de Chardin, *The Heart of the Matter*, trans. Rene Hague, (New York: Harcourt Brace Jovanovich, 1978), 121.

2. Rosemary Haughton, *The Passionate God*, 151.

3. Dorothee Soelle, *The Arms Race Kills*, trans. Gerhard A. Elston, (Philadelphia: Fortress Press, 1982), 16.

4. Charles Williams, *He Came Down from Heaven*, 86.

5. Vincent Donovan, *Christianity Rediscovered*, 59.

6. Helen Luke, *Dark Wood to White Rose*, 68.

7. Ruben Nelson, *Through the 80s*, ed. Frank Feather, (Washington, D.C.: World Future Society, 1980), 28.

8. Helen Luke, *Dark Wood to White Rose*, 44.

CHAPTER SIX

1. Kahlil Gibran, *The Prophet*, 69.

2. Charles Williams, *Greater Trumps*, (Grand Rapids: Eerdmans, 1976), 136.

3. Teilhard de Chardin, *The Divine Milieu*, 133.

4. Nelle Morton, *The Journey Is Home*, (Boston: Beacon Press, 1985), 227.

5. Dietrich Bonhoeffer, *Letters and Papers From Prison*, 212.

6. Dorothee Soelle, *Suffering*, trans. Everett R. Kalin, (Philadelphia: Fortress Press, 1975), 86.

7. Annie Dillard, *Holy the Firm*, 62.

8. William Stringfellow, *The Politics of Spirituality*, (Philadelphia: The Westminster Press, 1984), 84.

9. Dietrich Bonhoeffer, *Life Together*, trans. John W. Doberstein, (New York: Harper & Row, 1954), 86.

CHAPTER SEVEN

1. Sydney Carter, "The Lord of the Dance."

2. Attributed to Clarence Jordan.

3. Adapted from T.S. Eliot, *Four Quartets*, 28.

4. Daniel Berrigan, Introduction, *The Long Loneliness* by Dorothy Day, (San Francisco: Harper & Row, 1952), xxiii.

5. Annie Dillard, *Pilgrim at Tinker Creek*, (New York: Harper's Magazine Press, 1974), 276.

6. Teilhard de Chardin, *The Divine Milieu*, 128-9.

7. Teilhard de Chardin, *Hymn of the Universe*, trans. Simon Bartholomew, (New York: Harper & Row, 1965), 105.

8. Rubem Alves, *Tomorrow's Child*, (New York: Harper & Row, 1972), 204.

9. Robinson Jeffers, *The Selected Poetry of Robinson Jeffers*, (New York: Random House, 1938), 594.

10. Kahlil Gibran, *The Prophet*, 36-7.

11. Cesare Pavese, *This Business of Living: Diary 1935-50*, ed. and trans. A.E. Murch, (London: Peter Owen, Ltd., 1961), 151.

12. Maria Rainier Rilke, *Letters to a Young Poet*.

13. Annie Dillard, *Teaching a Stone to Talk*, 16.